THE TEACHING OF THE 12

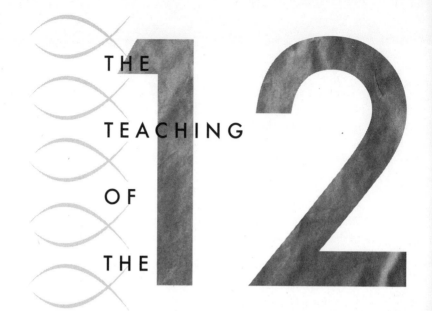

THE
TEACHING
OF
THE
12

believing & practicing
the primitive christianity
of the ancient didache
community

tony jones

PARACLETE PRESS
BREWSTER, MASSACHUSETTS

The Teaching of the Twelve: Believing and Practicing the Primitive Christianity of the Ancient Didache Community

2009 First Printing

ISBN 978-1-55725-590-7

Library of Congress Cataloging-in-Publication Data

Jones, Tony, 1968-

  The teaching of the twelve : believing and practicing the primitive Christianity of the ancient Didache community / Tony Jones.

    p. cm.

ISBN 978-1-55725-590-7 (pbk.)

1. Didache. 2. Christian ethics--History--Early church, ca. 30-600.
3. Church--History of doctrines--Early church, ca. 30-600. I. Title.

BS2940.T5J66 2009

270.1--dc22   2009043555

10 9 8 7 6 5 4 3 2 1

Published by Paraclete Press
Brewster, Massachusetts
www.paracletepress.com

Printed in the United States of America

Dedicated to Doug and Sarah Jones,

who trained me up in the way of the Lord

contents

preface

This has not been an easy book to write. For over a year I've read the Didache, alone, in groups, and with various online communities. I've read commentaries on it, and I've had extended conversations with New Testament scholars, church historians, and a couple of truck drivers. And, much to the chagrin of my longsuffering friends at Paraclete Press, I am long overdue at handing in the manuscript.

This is a fascinating little book, the Didache. And in the process of unpacking its history, the teaching therein exhibits extraordinary relevance to our own contemporary situation. When it comes to study, I'm an amateur polymath—I like the history, the theology, and the biblical study that the Didache conjures. So you'll find some of each of that in this book.

Far too often, academic work allows us to stay one (or more!) steps removed from our subject. Indeed, we're allowed and even taught to *objectify* the item of our study, to hold it at arm's distance. The personal implications of the study are rarely considered, except by the wizened emeritus professor, reflecting on a career well spent. But, growing up in the faith, the writers I admired most were Henri Nouwen and Frederick Buechner, men who combined theological acumen, pastoral experience, and deep introspection to produce beautiful, meaningful books on the Christian life.

It's in the shadows of these great writers, and others I've come to admire more recently (Phyllis Tickle and Barbara Brown Taylor among them), that I attempt to walk with this first-century text and community known as the Didache in *The Teaching of the Twelve*. A mysterious document—a glimpse into the most primitive Christianity—the Didache has challenged me for months now. I pray this book does honor to the anonymous Christ-followers who first penned this handbook of faith.

I offer my gratitude and thanks to my many friends at Paraclete Press and the Community of Jesus, primarily to Jon Sweeney and Pamela Jordan. Thanks to my agent, Kathy Helmers, for helping me map a literary trajectory. Thanks to Tim Owens for letting me read his Th.M. thesis on the Didache. And thanks to the many folks in my own community, Solomon's Porch, for thinking and praying through the Didache with me.

Special thanks are due to the Cymbrogi. In a way, the Didache community of the late first or early second century were pre-church. That is, they were gathering and deciding how to live in the Jesus Way before there really was any formal church structure as we know it today. While writing my last book, I met a small band of folks in rural Missouri who can only be considered post-church. Calling themselves the Cymbrogi—Celtic for "Companions of the

Heart"—they seek to live out a Christian community that is free of many of the trappings of modern church. When I told one of their number, whom we all call Trucker Frank, that I was writing a book on the Didache, he told me that the Cymbrogi had read the Didache together in their quest for a new perspective on faith—a new perspective from an ancient document. In fact, Frank himself had undertaken a thorough historical study of the text. I asked if they might journey through the book again with me, as I wrote, and they agreed. You will see more from them in coming pages, and read more about their community of faith in chapter 3. This book is immensely richer as a result of their partnership.

My heartfelt thanks to my children, too, whom I love more than life itself.

And, to my parents, to whom this book is dedicated: I love you.

—Tony Jones

THE TEACHING OF THE 12

1
The Most Important Book You've Never Heard Of

The Didache is the most important book you've never heard of.

In short, this strange, short handbook is a guide to living the Jesus Way in a very early Christian community. Who exactly wrote it, we're not sure. And when it was authored, we also don't quite know.

But what we can surmise is that the Didache (DID-ah-kay) records for us a most primitive Christianity, written about the same time as the synoptic Gospels (Matthew, Mark, and Luke) and before the Gospel of John; between the birth of the church (at Pentecost) and the official imprimatur of the emperor on the church (with the Edict of Milan in AD 313). Maybe most interestingly, the Didache records a Christianity seemingly unfamiliar with the theology and writings of the Apostle Paul.

This puts the Didache in an elite company. We have very few documents from the very early days of the church—the short era between the apostolic age, known to us from the biblical letters of Paul, Peter, John, and Hebrews, and the era of the ante-Nicene fathers, those churchmen such as Tertullian and Origen whose work predated the conversion of the emperor Constantine (AD 313) and the watershed Council of Nicaea (AD 325). What documents we *do* have from the turning of the first century of the common era into the second are primarily apocryphal, Gnostic writings, long since rejected as not reflective of the life of the burgeoning orthodox Christian church. Ultimately, no other work outside of the Bible is as early as the Didache, making it a unique text in the history of Christianity.

The early Christians were a small, if growing, band of believers, spreading across the Roman Empire. A blend of educated and uneducated, female and male, poor and rich, slaves and free, Jew and Gentile, just as the Apostle Paul had hoped, they had to keep their religion under wraps.

One of the elements that had contributed to the unprecedented Pax Romana—a period of relative peace in the empire, between 27 BC and AD 180—was that all religions were allowed, with one caveat: no matter one's religion, everyone in the empire still needed to pay the annual poll tax and declare the divinity of the Caesar. Both Jews and the new Christians chafed under the imperial cult, being that they were strident monotheists—paying the tax was one thing, but stating that the emperor was divine was beyond galling to them.

As a result of this, the burgeoning Christian church tried not to attract too much attention to themselves, though they did suffer several persecutions as various emperors blamed them for the troubles of the empire. Thus, outside of the canon of the New Testament, few documents have survived from this era of the early church. Seminarians often hear of these few in the first week of early church history class: *The Shepherd of Hermas, The Epistles of Clement of Rome, The Epistle of Barnabas, The Apocalypse of Peter,* and the Didache.

But, although it stands in this august company, the Didache receives far less attention than any of the books of the New Testament, simply for the fact that it is not considered sacred by the church. When the New Testament canon was closed, several centuries after Jesus' life, the books that made it into the Bible were destined for a readership in the billions, and those that were not were relegated to dusty seminary libraries—a cliché that is actually true of the Didache. As such, it remains largely unknown to Christians who have not studied the early church.

Yet it is—and I hope you will agree—a treatise that deserves a much wider readership.

The Long, Strange Journey of the Didache

In 1873, a forty-year-old archbishop was browsing through the library at the Greek Convent in the massive Church of the Holy Sepulchre in Istanbul when he came across a little book of 120 pages of parchment and a leather cover. In a library full of dusty, ancient texts, the book seemed unexceptional. Archbishop Philotheos Brynnios took the book with him back to his office with the intent to figure out what, exactly, it was, but his ecclesial duties pressed in on him, and when he told other scholars of his find, they, too, were unimpressed. It was several years before he turned his attention again to the book, and looking closely at it, he realized that he had something incredible in his hands.

What lay there on the archbishop's desk was an unknown and forgotten treasure of the earliest Christians, a manual for living used by the generation of Jesus followers immediately after the apostles. Modern scholars knew that it had once existed, for the Didache is mentioned in other ancient texts. Origen (AD 185–254) and Athanasius (AD 293–373) both wrote that it should not be included in the Bible, for it was just too local in its content, while other church fathers argued for its inclusion. Fifteen centuries later, scholars had resigned themselves to the fact that the Didache, like so many other ancient treasures, had been lost for good.

In 1882, nine years after it was discovered, another scholar, Adam Krawutzcky, was studying another ancient text, and it became clear to him—and he subsequently proved—that the text he was studying, written around AD 400, was in fact based on the little book discovered by the archbishop.

Now they knew that they had something special on their hands, and they rushed it to publication. The discovery of the Didache was an overnight sensation on both sides of the Atlantic; the day it was released, it sold over five thousand copies in New York City alone. Some hailed it as a lost treasure, while naysayers considered it a modern forgery, saying that it was not as authentic as the contemporaneously discovered Epistle of Barnabas. The former group prevailed, however, and the Didache is now unanimously considered one of the most important documents in the history of Christianity.

What Is It?

The leatherbound book that Archbishop Brynnios found in 1873 had been produced 817 years earlier, for it was signed by a long-forgotten monk, "Leon, scribe and sinner, 11 June 1056." As was common in the Middle Ages, many monks spent their days copying by hand the theological and philosophical treatises of the ancient world, and Brother Leon's mundane obedience produced a text that found its way onto the shelf of a monastery library and sat there, undiscovered, for eight centuries.

The whole text is just 2,190 words in Greek—that's less than half the length of the shortest of the four Gospels. It begins with a title, "Didache of the Twelve Apostles," and subtitle, "Didache of the Lord through the Twelve Apostles to the Gentiles."

The word *didache* is Greek and means "teaching." Contemporary words like *didactic* and *doctrine* come from the same root. Although today we capitalize it as the title of a book, the original manuscript, which we don't have, wouldn't have had any capital letters. In fact, it wouldn't have had any punctuation or spaces between words.

Various forms of the word *didache* are used a couple dozen times in the New Testament, often like in this verse in Matthew: "And when the crowd heard it, they were astonished at his teaching." In fact, this is the most common use of *didache* in the New Testament, referring to Jesus' teaching. In the Didache, Jesus is rarely mentioned, and *didache* lacks the pronoun *his* and thus is best translated as "the teaching." But the Didache does seem to assume throughout that the reader understands that Jesus is the progenitor of the teaching.

The Didache can be segmented in several ways. Some scholars see four natural sections, while others see six, and yet others see five. Although some scholars think of the Didache as the work of a single author, the consensus is that the "didachist" was more of an editor, stitching together four previous documents, a common practice in the ancient world, and not considered plagiarism by our modern standards. Those four sections are: the moral teaching drawn from a Jewish document known as "The Two Ways" (chapters 1–6); a liturgical treatise (chapters 7–10); a church organization treatise (chapters 11–15); and an apocalyptic section (chapter 16).

Here are the four sections in more detail:

1. Training in the Way of Life (1:1–6:2). Beginning with the now-famous and stark line, "There are two ways, one of life and one of death! and there is a great difference between the two ways," the opening section of the Didache is also the longest. This section is a detailed account of how a catechumen (or convert) to Christianity is to live and behave prior to her or his baptism. This section of the Didache has also been found as a fragment in other ancient documents, and most scholars agree that it is based on an earlier Jewish document.

2. The Rhythms of Community Life (6:3–11:2). In the second section, the Didache community takes up the various regulations for followers of the Way after they are baptized and have joined the church. Rules for eating, baptizing, fasting, praying, and sharing the Lord's Supper are all addressed.

3. Visitors Welcome (11:3–15:4). The third section of the Didache addresses various regulations regarding visitors to the community. Most of the time is spent on wandering prophets and teachers who come with wisdom, and occasionally with earthly requests for food and money. While hospitality is vaunted, limits are also imposed. Next, the community again addresses the Eucharist, further exhorting community members to cleanse both their hands and their consciences prior to partaking. The criteria for choosing community leaders is also explicated.

4. The End Is Nigh (16:1–8). Finally, as with the New Testament, the Didache concludes with an apocalyptic section. The community is warned to prepare for the end of time, and they're told the signs that will indicate the end.

It's as though the members of the Didache community took several short pamphlets on the Christian life and bound them together for use as a handbook. More specifically, it can be considered a "rule of life" for the Didache community. More commonly known from its later use in monastic communities (for instance, with the Benedictines), a rule of life is a book of precepts used by all who submit themselves to some form of community. In other words, the Didache is fundamentally *practical*. And just as it guided the earliest Christians in their daily practice of faith, it is now attracting the attention of many who desire to learn from the earliest followers of Jesus about their way of life. For the first 150 years since the Didache's rediscovery, it has been primarily the purview of academics. But the time has come for this ancient document to inspire its intended audience: those starting out in their faith.

Drawing primarily from Jewish-Christian sources, the Didache seems to be particularly for non-Jews (Gentiles) and Hellenized Jews who had converted to Christianity and were joining the community of Jewish-Christians. The text—particularly chapters 1–5 ("The Two Ways")—was circulated fairly widely in the early church, leading to its many references in other ancient documents. But, as Christianity grew and became the dominant religion in the empire, the Didache's popularity waned. For one thing, the Didache contains no mention of clergy or priesthood, nor does it grant bishops ecclesiastical authority, so it wouldn't have been a very popular book for the burgeoning church hierarchy in the fourth and fifth centuries. Secondly, the Didache's version of the Lord's Supper liturgy is dramatically different than that of Paul's direction in 1 Corinthians; in the

Didache, there is no mention of Jesus' death on the cross as the reason for Communion, and the traditional order of bread and cup is reversed, putting it at odds with even the earliest liturgies of the church.

Finally, the Didache is a book entirely consumed with a Christianity that is both everyday and ordinary. It lacks Paul's interest in complex doctrine and reflects none of the early church's predilection for proclaiming the heavenly titles and deeds of Christ. The cosmic Christ of John's Gospel is nowhere to be found in the Didache, nor are the apostolic miracles found in the Acts of the Apostles. Instead, it is a book interested in other simpler things: how to know right from wrong, how to baptize one another, and how to treat visiting preachers.

Our last known reference to the Didache in other Christian writings comes from Patriarch Nicephoros of Constantinople. He listed it among a list of apocryphal books. That was in the 820s.

After that, the Didache was silent for over one thousand years.

When Was It Written? And By Whom?

The date and author of the Didache have been debated for years. When it was first rediscovered, most experts thought it surely must have come from the late second, or even early third, century. But over time, that opinion has changed considerably. Currently, there are two major camps: one group of scholars dates the Didache at AD 110–130; the other group dates it between AD 50 and 70. For the sake of comparison, most New Testament scholars date the letters of Paul in the 50s, the synoptic Gospels (Matthew, Mark, and Luke) between 60 and 110, and the Gospel of John around 110.

The reasons for this early date are various, but they mainly have to do with both the context and the style of writing in the Didache. Further, the authors seemingly had no familiarity with either the letters of Paul or with John's Gospel, which would be increasingly unlikely in the second century. In the end, the Didache is, as I have said, the record of a primitive Christianity, a glimpse into the lives of some of the earliest followers of Jesus. So let's put it this way: portions of the Didache were written a couple of decades after Jesus' crucifixion, and in the version we have it, the book was compiled very early in the second century.

Where these Jesus followers lived is even more mysterious. Some think Egypt, since that's where several of the earliest manuscripts have been found. Others argue for Syria, based on the writing style, the allusions to mountains and hills, and the lack of running water mentioned in the baptismal regulations. Still others say that Palestine, or the Syria-Palestine, border is most likely due to the Didache's similarities with the Gospel of Matthew. In fact, each of the New Testament Gospels—Matthew, Mark, Luke, and John—was written to a particular geographical and ethnic audience, and has theological distinctives that betray that audience. In this sense, the Didache is no different.

We can say with relative confidence that the Didache was used by a community of Christians who lived in a relatively rural area, and who were a mixture of Jews and Gentiles who had converted to the Way of Jesus. Although the title, which was probably added later, notes that this book contains the teaching of the twelve apostles, that doesn't mean they authored it. It was common practice in the ancient world to attribute a work to an author or authors who would lend credibility to the document. So instead of being authored by the apostles, the Didache is a distillation of their teachings, the teachings of the earliest church.

Some Notes for Reading

Most likely, you'll be reminded of the Bible when you start to read the Didache—specifically, it will remind you of Matthew's Gospel (we'll talk about this more in chapter 3). When possible, try to free yourself from the preconceptions that you carry about the Bible, and try to remind yourself that the Didache is a similar, but different, kind of document.

The first suggestion I have for you is to *read slowly*. From the earliest days of Christianity, the process of "sacred reading" (*lectio divina*) has been practiced by Jesus followers. I encourage you to try this with the following chapter, which houses the entire text of the Didache. Read it at about half the speed that you've read this chapter. If you find your mind wandering, gently stop, regain your concentration, and go back to reading.

Second, remember to whom the Didache was written, and try to read it from their perspective. To the Didache's original readers, Jesus' death and resurrection was within recent history—even memory. They were converts to Christianity, either from Judaism or from Roman paganism. And, most significantly, remember that those readers didn't have the Bible as we know it; they knew the Hebrew Scriptures (Old Testament), but much of the New Testament had not yet been written—the stories that we know from the New Testament, they knew because they had been passed by word of mouth from town to town. At most, they had read or heard the Gospels of Matthew and Luke; more likely, they had heard stories from those Gospels before those Gospels were finally composed.

Finally, don't get hung up on the chapter and verse numbers and the subtitles. They've been added to help us as modern readers, but they weren't in the original document. If you find them helpful, use them. If you find them an annoyance, ignore them.

I've used indentations and extra spaces to indicate my thoughts of how best to read the Didache and to notify the reader about sections that most likely went together originally. And I've bracketed two verses (4:1 and 10:7) that I consider later additions to the text.

But Most Important . . .

What you are about to read is an unparalleled glimpse into the earliest Christianity. As I said, it may immediately remind you of a part of the Bible, and you may be tempted to treat it as passé for that reason. But don't. That would be a mistake.

For the Didache offers something of an alternative to what many know of Christianity. The real power of the Didache is its ability to remind us what is truly important in Christianity: showing the love of Jesus to the world.

The people who wrote and compiled the Didache were just figuring this out. They must have been confused, and they were probably scared. They had little to go on other than some stories about Jesus, maybe a letter or two from a nearby church, and a fresh experience of God's liberating Spirit.

At first, it might be difficult to see this in the Didache. You might instead see a pretty simple handbook that seems similar to the Bible. But you've got to read between the lines a bit and imagine what was really going on in those days as Christianity spread, slowly and illegally, across the empire. And you may have to temporarily set aside some patterns and traditions that Christianity has picked up in the two millennia between the Didache and today. Of course, that's not easy, because ours is the only Christianity that we know.

But, in the end, we have a lot to learn from those long-departed, early saints of the church—they call out to us from a little desert village outside of Antioch, in the late first century. They have something important to tell us, if only we will listen.

Thoughts from Trucker Frank

At the end of each chapter, I'll recount a pertinent portion of my conversation with Trucker Frank about how he and the Cymbrogi have applied the Didache to their own community.

In the Cymbrogi, "Everyone has grown up with modern interpretations," Frank told me. They'd been reared in families and churches where words like *church* and *pastor* had definite meanings, so when they ran across words like that in the Bible or in their communities of faith, they naturally assented to the conventional meanings of those words. "When we discovered the Didache," Frank said, "we realized that these were new things in that day. Everything was new to them, and the Didache captured our desire to get back to a Christianity without the doctrines and creeds." Frank continued, "All the people in the Didache community had was this person Jesus who had lived an extraordinary life and died an extraordinary death. That's all they had." What I think Frank meant was that, although the people in the Didache community were likely versed in Jewish theology and Greek philosophy, they didn't have much Christian theology yet. What they had, instead, was a powerful, life-altering experience with the Lord Jesus. They were left trying to figure out what it meant to live a life worthy of that Lord, and the Didache is their attempt to do just that.

Questions for Reflection, Study, and Discussion

1. The Cymbrogi appreciate the early date of the Didache and feel that it adds to their understanding of the Bible. Is it a new idea to you that there were other texts written at the same time as the New Testament books that weren't

included in the New Testament? How does that change your understanding of the New Testament? How does the early date of the Didache affect your perception of the book? Does it make you think it's particularly important?

2. Think of a book or two that altered your perception of God and/or Jesus? What was it about that book that affected you?

3. When you turn the page, you'll begin reading the Didache, maybe for the first time. Before you dive into it, what are your thoughts, apprehensions, and expectations?

2

The Didache, or The Teaching of the Twelve Apostles

THE COMPLETE TEXT

1 There Are Two Ways

1:1 There are two ways, one of life and one of death!
and there is a great difference between the two ways.

1:2 The way of life is this:

First, you shall love God who made you.

And second, love your neighbor as yourself, and do not
do to another what you would not want done to you.

1:3 The meaning of these sayings is this:

Bless those who curse you, and pray for your enemies,
and fast for those who persecute you. For what reward
is there for loving those who love you? Do not the
heathens do the same? But you should love those who
hate you, and then you shall have no enemies.

1:4 Abstain from fleshly and bodily lusts:

If someone strikes your right cheek, turn the other
also, and be perfect. If someone forces you to go one
mile, go two. If someone takes your cloak, give also
your coat. If someone takes from you what is yours,
don't ask for it back. You really cannot.

1:5 Give to every one who asks you, and don't ask for it back. The Father wants his blessings shared.

Happy is the giver who lives according to this rule, for that one is guiltless. But the receiver must beware; for if one receives who has need, he is guiltless, but if one receives not having need, he shall stand trial, answering why he received and for what use. If he is found guilty he shall not escape until he pays back the last penny.

1:6 However, concerning this, there is a saying: "Let your alms sweat in your hands until you know to whom to give them."

2 **The Second Commandment**

2:1 The second commandment of the teaching is this:

2:2 Do not commit murder;

do not commit adultery;

do not corrupt boys;

do not have illicit sex;

do not steal;

do not practice magic;

do not practice witchcraft;

you shall not murder a child,

whether it be born or unborn.

Do not covet the things of your neighbor.

2:3 Do not swear or bear false witness.

Do not speak evil of others; do not bear grudges.

2:4 You should not be double-minded or double-tongued, for a double-tongue is a deadly snare.

2:5 Your speech should not be false nor empty, but fulfilled by action.

2:6 Do not be covetous, or greedy, or hypocritical, or malicious, or arrogant.

Do not have designs against your neighbor.

2:7 Hate no one;

correct some, pray for others, and some you should love more than your own life.

3 My Child, Flee Evil

3:1 My child, flee evil of all kinds, and everything like it.

3:2 Don't be prone to anger, for anger leads to murder. Don't be jealous or quarrelsome or hot-tempered, for all these things lead to murder.

3:3 My child, don't be lustful, for lust leads to illicit sex. Don't be a filthy talker or allow your eyes a free reign, for these lead to adultery.

3:4 My child, don't observe omens, since it leads to idolatry. Don't be an enchanter, or an astrologer, or a purifier, or be willing to see or hear about these things, for these all lead to idolatry.

3:5 My child, don't be a liar, since a lie leads to theft. Don't love money or seek glory, for these things lead to thievery.

3:6 My child, don't grumble, since it leads to blasphemy, and don't be self-willed or evil-minded, for all these things lead to blasphemy.

3:7 On the contrary, be gentle, since the gentle will inherit the earth.

3:8 Be long-suffering and pitiful and guileless and gentle and good, and with trembling, treasure the words you have received.

3:9 Don't exalt yourself or open your heart to over-confidence. Don't be on intimate terms with mighty people, but with just and lowly ones.

3:10 Accept whatever happens to you as a blessing, knowing that nothing comes to pass apart from God.

4   My Child, Remember

[4:1 My child, remember day and night him who speaks the word of God to you, and honor him as the Lord. For wherever his lordship is spoken of, there he is.]

4:2 Seek each day the faces of the saints, in order that you may be refreshed by their words.

4:3 Do not initiate divisions, but rather bring peace to those who contend against one another. Judge righteously, and do not take social status into account when reproving for transgressions.

4:4 Do not waver in your decisions.

4:5 Do not be one who opens his hands to receive, or closes them when it is time to give.

4:6 If you have anything, by your hands you should give ransom for your sins.

4:7 Do not hesitate to give, and do not complain about it. You will know in time who is the good Rewarder.

4:8 Do not turn away from one who is in want; rather, share all things with your brother, and do not say that they are your own. For if you are sharers in what is imperishable, how much more in things which perish!

4:9 Do not remove your hand from your son or daughter; teach them the fear of God from their youth.

4:10 Do not give orders to your servants when you are angry, for they hope in the same God, and they may lose the fear of God, who is over both of you. God is surely not coming to call on us according to our outward appearance or station in life, but to them whom the Spirit has prepared.

4:11 And you, servants, be subject to your masters as to God's image, in modesty and fear.

4:12 You should hate all hypocrisy and everything which is not pleasing to the Lord.

> **4:13** Do not in any way neglect the commandments of the Lord, but keep what you have received, neither adding nor taking away anything.

> **4:14** In your gatherings, confess your transgressions, and do not come for prayer with a guilty conscience.

This is the way of life!

5   The Way of Death

5:1 The way of death, on the other hand, is this:

It is evil and accursed—murders, adulteries, lust, illicit sex, thefts, idolatries, magical arts, sorceries, robberies, false testimonies, hypocrisy, double-heartedness, deceit, haughtiness, depravity, self-will, greediness, filthy talking, jealousy, over-confidence, loftiness, boastfulness—those who do not fear God.

5:2 The way of death is the way of those who persecute the good, hate the truth, love lies, and do not understand the reward for righteousness.

> They do not cleave to good or righteous judgment; they do not watch for what is good, but for what is evil.

> They are strangers to meekness and patience, loving vanities, pursuing revenge, without pity for the needy and oppressed.

They do not know their Creator; they are murderers of
children, destroyers of God's image.

They turn away from those who are in need, making
matters worse for those who are distressed.

They are advocates for the rich, unjust judges of the
poor.

In a word, the way of death is full of those who are
steeped in sin.

Be delivered, children, from all of this!

6   See That No One Leads You Astray

6:1   See that no one leads you astray from the way of this
teaching, since all other teachings train you without
God.

> **6:2**   For if you are able to bear the entire yoke of the
> Lord, you will be perfect; but if you are not able,
> then at least do what you can.

> **6:3**   Concerning food, do what you are able to do and be
> on guard against meat offered to idols, for that is to
> worship dead gods.

7   Concerning Baptism

7:1   Concerning baptism, you should baptize this way:

After first explaining all things, baptize in the name
of the Father, and of the Son, and of the Holy Spirit, in
flowing water.

7:2   But if you have no running water, baptize in other
water; and if you cannot do so in cold water, then in
warm.

7:3   If you have very little, pour water three times on the
head in the name of Father and Son and Holy
Spirit.

7:4   Before the baptism, both the baptizer and the
candidate for baptism, plus any others who can,
should fast. The candidate should fast for one or two
days beforehand.

8   Your Fasts and Prayers

8:1   Your fasts should not be with the hypocrites, for
they fast on Mondays and Thursdays. You should fast
on Wednesdays and Fridays.

8:2   And do not pray like the hypocrites, but rather as the
Lord commanded in the gospel:
Our Father in heaven, holy be your name. Your kingdom
come. Your will be done, on earth as it is in heaven. Give
us enough bread day-by-day. And forgive us our debts, as
we also have forgiven our debtors. And do not bring us to
the time of trial, but rescue us from the evil one.

8:3   Pray this three times each day.

9 **Concerning the Eucharist**

9:1 Concerning the Eucharist, give thanks this way.

> **9:2** First, concerning the cup:
> We thank you, our Father, for the holy vine of David your servant, which you made known to us through Jesus your servant. To you be the glory forever.
>
> **9:3** Next, concerning the broken bread:
> We thank you, our Father, for the life and knowledge which you made known to us through Jesus your servant. To you be the glory forever.
>
> **9:4** Even as this broken bread was scattered over the hills, and was gathered together and became one, so let your church be gathered together from the ends of the earth into your kingdom. To you is the glory and the power through Jesus Christ forever.
>
> **9:5** Allow no one to eat or drink of your Eucharist, unless they have been baptized in the name of the Lord. For concerning this, the Lord has said, "Do not give what is holy to dogs."

10 **After the Eucharist**

10:1 After the Eucharist when you are filled, give thanks this way:

> **10:2** We thank you, holy Father, for your holy name which you enshrined in our hearts, and for the knowledge and faith and immortality that you

made known to us through Jesus your servant. To
you be the glory forever.

10:3 You, Master Almighty, have created all things
for your name's sake. You gave food and drink to all
people for enjoyment, that they might give thanks
to you; but to us you freely give spiritual food and
drink and life eternal through Jesus, your servant.

10:4 Before all things we thank you because you are
mighty. To you be the glory forever.

10:5 Remember, Lord, your church. Deliver it from all
evilandmakeitperfectinyourlove,andgatheritfrom
thefourwindssanctifiedforyourkingdomwhichyou
have prepared for it. For Yours is the power and the
glory forever.

10:6 Let grace come, and let this world pass away!
Hosanna to the Son of David! If anyone is holy,
let him come; if anyone is not holy, let him
repent. Maranatha!
Amen.

[**10:7** But permit the prophets to make thanksgiving as much
as they desire.]

11   Welcome the Teacher

11:1 Welcome the teacher when he comes to instruct you in
all that has been said.

11:2 But if he turns and trains you in another tradition to the destruction of this teaching, do not listen. If he teaches so as to increase righteousness and the knowledge of the Lord, receive him as the Lord.

11:3 Act according to the precepts of the gospel concerning all apostles and prophets:

11:4 Let every apostle who comes to you be received as the Lord.

11:5 But he must not remain more than one day, or two, if there's a need. If he stays three days, he is a false prophet.

11:6 And when the apostle goes away, let him take nothing but bread to last him until his next night of lodging. If he asks for money, he is a false prophet.

11:7 In addition, if any prophet speaks in the Spirit, you shall not try or judge him; for every sin will be forgiven, but this sin cannot be forgiven.

11:8 But not everyone who speaks in the Spirit is a prophet; only he is a prophet who has the ways of the Lord about him. By their ways will the false prophet and the prophet be known.

11:9 Any prophet who orders a meal in the Spirit does not eat it; if he does, he is indeed a false prophet.

11:10 And any prophet who teaches the truth, but does not do what he teaches, is a false prophet.

11:11 When a prophet, proved true, works for the mystery of the church in the world but does not teach others to do what he himself does, he will not be judged among you, for his judgment is already before God. The ancient prophets acted in this way, also.

11:12 But whoever says in the Spirit, "Give me money," or something else like this, you must not listen to him. But if he tells you to give for the sake of others who are in need, let no one judge him.

12   Welcome Anyone Coming in the Name of the Lord

12:1 Welcome anyone coming in the name of the Lord. Receive everyone who comes in the name of the Lord, but then, test them and use your discretion.

12:2 If he who comes is a transient, assist him as far as you are able; but he should not remain with you more than two or three days, if need be.

12:3 If he wants to stay with you, and is a craftsman, let him work for his living.

12:4 But if he has no trade, use your judgment in providing for him; for a Christian should not live idle in your midst.

12:5 If he is dissatisfied with this sort of an arrangement, he is a Christ peddler. Watch that you keep away from such people.

13   Every Genuine Prophet

13:1 Every genuine prophet who wants to live among you is worthy of support.

> **13:2** So also, every true teacher is, like a workman, entitled to his support.
>
> **13:3** Every first fruit, therefore, of the products of vintage and harvest, of cattle and of sheep, should be given as first fruits to the prophets, for they are your high priests.
>
> **13:4** But if you have no prophet, give it all to the poor.
>
> **13:5** If you bake bread, take the first loaf and give it according to the commandment.
>
> **13:6** If you open a new jar of wine or of oil, take the first fruit and give it to the prophets.
>
> **13:7** If you acquire money or cloth or any other possession, set aside a portion first, as it may seem good to you, and give according to the commandment.

14   On the Lord's Day

14:1 On the Lord's day, gather yourselves together and break bread, give thanks, but first confess your sins so that your sacrifice may be pure.

14:2 However, let no one who is at odds with his brother come together with you, until he has reconciled, so that your sacrifice may not be profaned.

14:3 For this is what the Lord has said: "For from the rising of the sun to its setting my name is great among the nations, and in every place incense is offered to my name, and a pure offering; for my name is great among the nations, says the LORD of hosts. . . . For I am a great King, says the LORD of hosts, and my name is reverenced among the nations."

15   Appoint Bishops for Yourselves

15:1 Appoint bishops for yourselves, as well as deacons, worthy of the Lord, of meek disposition, unattached to money, truthful and proven; for they also render to you the service of prophets and teachers.

15:2 Do not despise them, after all, for they are your honored ones, together with the prophets and teachers.

15:3 And reprove one another, not in anger, but in peace, as you have it in the gospel. But to anyone who acts amiss against another, let no one speak to him, nor let him hear anything from you until he repents. But your prayers and alms and all your deeds so do, as you have it in the gospel of our Lord.

16   Watch Over Your Life

16:1 Watch over your life, that your lamps are never quenched, and that your loins are never unloosed. Be ready, for you do not know on what day your Lord is coming.

16:2 Come together often, seeking the things that are good for your souls. A life of faith will not profit you if you are not made perfect at the end of time.

16:3 For in the last days false prophets and corrupters will be plenty, and the sheep will be turned into wolves, and love will be turned into hate.

16:4 When lawlessness increases, they will hate and persecute and betray one another, and then the world-deceiver will appear claiming to be the Son of God, and he will do signs and wonders, and the earth will be delivered into his hands, and he will do iniquitous things that have not been seen since the beginning of the world.

16:5 Then humankind will enter into the fire of trial, and many will be made to stumble and many will perish; but those who endure in their faith will be saved from under the curse itself.

16:6 And then the signs of the truth will appear: the first sign, an opening of the heavens; the second sign, the sounding of the trumpet; and the third sign, the resurrection of the dead—

16:7 not of every one, but as it is said: "Then the LORD my God will come, and all the holy ones with him."

16:8 Finally, "Then the sign of the Son of Man will appear in heaven, and then all the tribes of the earth will mourn, and they will see 'the Son of Man coming on the clouds of heaven' with power and great glory."

Questions for Reflection, Study, and Discussion

Record your initial reactions to reading the Didache. What surprised you? What did you appreciate most? What did you find confusing?

3
The Didache Community— Then and Now

In AD 70, or AD 110, Christianity really wasn't the Christianity that we know today. First, it was primarily considered a sect of Judaism. Jesus had been called a rabbi during his life, as we frequently read in the Gospels. Those who continued to follow his teachings, and to believe in his messiahship, after his death and resurrection were called "followers of the Way" or "Nazarenes" (since Jesus was from Nazareth) in the early days; in the Acts of the Apostles, we learn that followers in Antioch—near the Didache community—were the first to be called "Christians."

The lines between Christians and Jews were more fuzzy than distinct in the early days. There were Jews who thought that Jesus was the Messiah, and Jews who thought that the Messiah was yet to come. Some synagogues had become Nazarene synagogues, and others had not. The Gospel of Matthew feels very Jewish friendly, while the Gospel of John does not. In fact, some scholars have suggested that what comes across as anti-Judaism in John's Gospel is actually a form of "fraternal name-calling"—that is, these were among the early, intramural fights for the heart of the new version of Judaism. Christianity began as a sect of Judaism, not as its own, discrete religion.

As you might imagine, traditional synagogues cared little for Nazarene synagogues and the nascent "house churches" (*domus ecclesiae*) emerging among Christians. In fact, the conflict between traditional Jews and Jesus-following Jews led to the expulsion of all Jews from Rome in AD 49. Two more momentous events took place in the second half of the first century: the Roman general Titus sacked and destroyed the Temple in Jerusalem in 70, and the emperor Nerva exempted Christians from the extra tax that was levied upon Jews. The former event led to a significant change in Judaism—with the loss of the Temple, local synagogue worship took on much greater significance. And the latter opened Christians up to persecution since they were no longer considered Jews, and Judaism was a protected religion during the Pax Romana.

While we don't know the exact date of the Didache (whether it was written before or after the fall of the Temple) or the exact place that it was written, we can surmise that the Hellenized Jewish Christians (Jews who lived away from Jerusalem and were culturally Greek and Greek speaking) in the Didache community knew that they were living in turbulent times. What exactly it meant to be Christian was still being sorted out: Were they still Jewish, or not? Were they to obey the laws of Torah, or not? What was their relationship to Judaism? To Rome? To other churches? Meanwhile, Paul, of whom the Didache takes no notice, was arguing with Peter over the relationship between Gentile Christians and Jewish Christians.

The first few centuries of Christianity were often frightening times for converts to the new sect. The Roman emperor Nero launched a persecution of Christians in Rome in 64, blaming Nazarenes for the great fire that razed much of the city. That persecution lasted for four years, but other persecutions sprang up around the empire, whenever it became convenient to blame Christians for something. It wouldn't be until the emperor Constantine, following his own conversion, issued the Edict of Milan in 313 that Christianity became legal and tolerated.

All this to say that the Christians of the Didache community weren't wearing crosses around their necks or affixing fish stickers to the backs of their chariots.

Because the Didache was written in Greek, we can assume that, like the Gospels and Paul's letters, it was meant for Jews in the "Diaspora"—that is, Jews who lived outside of Jerusalem. These Jews likely used the Septuagint, a Greek translation of the Hebrew Scripture. (Jesus and his disciples most likely spoke in the Aramaic language and probably used the Targum.) Considering this, and some of the geographical references in the Didache, it's probable that it was compiled for a Nazarene synagogue in Syria—probably near Antioch—and specifically for those who were converting to Nazarene Judaism from paganism.

So, here's the bottom line: although we can't be certain about the community that compiled and used the Didache, we can make some educated guesses. They lived outside of the heart of Judaism, Jerusalem, probably in a rural area on the Syria-Palestine border; they were Greek-speaking Jews who had converted to Christianity; they developed the Didache as a manual to assist non-Jews (gentiles) in their conversion to Christianity; and all this is in the context of the second half of the first century, a time when Christianity was growing at an exciting rate, but amid much struggle and persecution.

What we can assume—and will from this point forward—is that the Didache was written to a specific, discrete community at a particular point in time. All we know of them is what we can surmise from the Didache and from our knowledge about the very earliest Christians. For lack of a better term, we will refer to them as the "Didache community."

We do know this: they were new converts to a new religion, attempting to figure out what it all meant.

A Didache Community, Maysville, MO 64469

In rural Missouri, about an hour outside of Kansas City, a small group of eight to ten Christians meets each week. Disillusioned with church-as-usual, the group consists of a small business owner, a cattle farmer, a state government worker, a homeschooling mom, a medical worker, a sales representative, a retired widow, a title company supervisor, a builder, and two truck drivers. They're former Lutherans, Baptists, Methodists, and Mennonites. And they call themselves the Cymbrogi (koom-BRO-gee), which is Celtic for "Companions of the Heart."

One of the group's members, Frank Schutzwohl, and I have become friends over the past couple years. Better known as "Trucker Frank," he is an autodidact who teaches a Greek class to his fellow Cymbrogi. When Frank heard of my interest in the Didache, he told me that the Cymbrogi were interested in it, too. More specifically, they were in search of a "pre-Ignatian Christianity," in Trucker Frank's words.

He went on to explain to me that Ignatius of Antioch was an apostolic father—that is, he was among the generation of theologians and church leaders in the generation immediately following the apostles—and, according to the early church historian Eusebius, Ignatius followed St. Peter and St. Evodius as the third bishop of Antioch. Today, we have seven letters written by Ignatius, all of them to other churches, around the end of the first century.

One of the main battles of his day was Gnosticism, a strong influence in many ancient religions that emphasized a "secret knowledge" available to the person who did and believed the right things. Ignatius struggled against Gnosticism both theologically and politically, and it's the latter that bothers Trucker Frank. In order to fight back the influence of Gnosticism in the early church, Ignatius advocated a church hierarchy more strict than any that had previously been used. Whereas letters by other apostolic fathers imply that a church could have several bishops, presbyters, and deacons, Ignatius makes the chain of command clear: there is to be one bishop per city, and that bishop is in authority over the other church leaders.

While Ignatius's motive of battling Gnosticism was noble, Trucker Frank and the Cymbrogi struggle with his institutionalization of church hierarchy. They're a small, group—a house church, really—and many of them have turned away from structured church. So they've been on a quest for a pre-Ignatian Christianity, one that is more reflective of their understanding of the Christianity of the New Testament.

Although theirs is an egalitarian fellowship, Trucker Frank does bring some theological training to the Cymbrogi.

A graduate of Bible college, Frank took up preaching at an early age. But he also ran into problems with church politics, and he was run out of a couple of churches, always for being a bit too brazen in the pulpit—for instance, he was once fired as a pastor for comparing the congregation to the artificial potted plants on the platform during a sermon. Frank ultimately settled in as a school bus driver and then an over-the-road trucker.

But Frank's profession hasn't kept him—or the rest of the Cymbrogi for that matter—from furthering their theological education. Frank has a library of theological commentaries that would put many professional pastors to shame, and he regularly studies the New Testament and other early Christian documents in the original Greek. This commitment to study and discipleship came after a rough patch in Frank's life that included a painful divorce, a suicide attempt, and some other unhealthy choices. Recovering from this period, Frank restarted his search for a primitive Christianity.

Many in the Cymbrogi have similar stories, which often include disenfranchisement from conventional church life. Surely disillusionment has been a part of each of their journeys and has been the motivation of their quest, of which the Didache has been a significant part. And what they have found—and how they've chosen to live—has provoked interest and criticism from many of their family and friends.

Growing up in conservative Christianity (first German Catholic, then fundamentalist Mennonite), Frank had often been warned against reading the non-canonical books of the early church. Whether they be the spurious Gospels of the second- and third-century Gnostics or the epistles of Polycarp and Clement, they were off limits to Frank when he was younger. He told me, "It's like when your parents tell you not to look at something, it makes you want to look all the more."

So with his burgeoning and broadening theology of late, Frank has been keen to consume the writings of the ante-Nicene church. And to Frank and the Cymbrogi, the Didache was a jewel of the faith that they didn't even know existed. They are, Frank thinks, among the items to which the writer of the fourth Gospel refers when he writes, "But there are also many other things that Jesus did; if every one of them were written down, I suppose that the world itself could not contain the books that would be written."

Another member of the Cymbrogi, Frank's ex-brother-in-law, Trucker John, likes the Didache, too. As the church grew in the first centuries, the emphasis became more and more on what you believe, which creed you recite, which doctrine you believe. But the Didache, John says, preserves a Christianity that emphasizes how you live. According to Trucker John, this seems more in keeping with the teachings of Jesus than the later controversies over doctrine ever did. At least it speaks to him in a way that he needed and found encouraging.

So the Cymbrogi read through the Didache for several weeks, and they put it in conversation with the rhythms of their own community life. They rarely meet as a whole group, but more often in groups of three or four; they connect with one another on the phone and on Facebook; they put their Christianity at the center of their lives. In my estimation, they exemplify one of the potential futures of Christianity, in which the faith is populated by small groups of outliers and renegades, disconnected from the bureaucracies of modern denominations but connecting with one another and with other like-minded communities through various media. But that is only one part of Christianity's future. The Didache also has much to teach those of us in more conventional church bodies. Whether our church experience is at a coffee shop or a mega-church, the Didache's vision of communal life in Christ is powerful and potentially transformative.

For the Cymbrogi, the Didache's primitive rhythms of faith have changed them personally. Each one of them I've spoken to has professed that the raw, organic Christianity that they found in the Didache and now attempt to practice is exactly what they'd been looking for all along. It's what they'd wanted out of a faith in Jesus, and now they have it.

They speak of feeling more connected to one another than in any other "church" they've ever been a part of. They report a depth of honesty that's extremely rare in our age, when communication is voluminous but rarely intimate. It's like they've put on the brakes. They don't talk about how to "grow their church." Instead, they study Greek together. They don't worry about paying someone to lead them and teach them. Instead, they all pitch in to the conversations about how to live faithfully.

What they're doing might not be replicable on a large scale—come to think if it, maybe that's why the Didache fell into disuse as Christianity (and the church hierarchy) grew. But all of us who endeavor to live faithfully as Christians in community with other Christians should at least pay heed to the Cymbrogi's experiment, for it might have powerful lessons even for the largest and oldest Christian churches.

Thoughts from Trucker Frank

If you come to the little town where the Cymbrogi live, there will be no signs on the street corner or listings in the phone book pointing you to their "church." "We met in a 'church building' at one time," Frank told me. "But we now meet in homes, cafes, and anywhere that two or three of us can gather together. I saw the term *Cymbrogi* in my reading and came to refer to our group in this way."

Since they have no membership, the people under the umbrella of this term are difficult to single out. And because they cross denominational lines and some are still involved in more conventional churches, they don't all meet together at the same time and in the same place. "What we share is a deep, soulful commitment to each other and to a fellowship beyond the walls of institutional church structures," Frank says. "We are sometimes viewed with suspicion by others because we refuse to stay within the boundaries of a particular church hierarchy. We are, in that sense, an organic structure somewhere between the local church and the Church Universal."

Questions for Reflection, Study, and Discussion

1. When reading about life for a first-century follower of Jesus, what was most surprising to you? When you think about the world of the first century, does it change how you read the Bible? The Didache?

2. Have you ever experienced any persecution for your faith close to the persecution of the early Christians? How would the faith of you and your family change if you lived in a country in which Christianity was forbidden?

3. Would you like to be a part of a Christian community like the Cymbrogi? What aspects of that community appeal to you, and what parts repel you?

4

There Are Two Ways

One of the hallmarks of today's world has got to be complexity. Many aspects of globalization have influenced the ways that we live, such as rapid, long-distance communication and global financial markets. But nothing has affected us like electronic communication. More raw information has been generated in the past decade than in the previous five thousand years of human history. In 2006, IBM released a white paper predicting that by 2010 (that's now!), the amount of digital information in the world will double every eleven hours; already, more electronic transistors are manufactured annually than grains of rice grown in the entire world.

But you probably don't need more statistics to impress upon you the massive amounts of information and data that have been produced by the advent of computing, mobile phones, and satellites. We're interested less in the phenomenon and more in the effects. Because, among other things, this has led to *gray*.

And by gray, I mean neither black nor white.

Just think of all those jokes about whether red meat, coffee, or red wine are good for you. One week there's a medical report in the news that says one of them will kill you, and the next week you'll read an article touting the medical benefits of the same item. It's maddening, and it's led many of us not to take many of these medical pronouncements seriously.

Or think of how often you've heard someone assert: "You can make the Bible say anything you want it to!" We are awash in a world of complexities, paradoxes, nuances, and gray.

So how odd to our ears to hear the Didache community say, from many centuries ago, that there are "two ways." Not many ways. And no middle way. Just two ways: a way of life and a way of death.

The complexities in our world lead us to think that there are many ways, or even a terabyte worth of ways to live—and not simply due to computer technology. It's also a legacy of the twentieth century, a time during which dictators regularly claimed to have The Way to live and The Truth about God and the universe. But when these claims were made, the inevitable result was that people died. Think Hitler and Pol Pot; think Jim Jones and David Koresh. Surely these were not the first abusive dictators and absolutist cult leaders in history, nor, sadly, will they be the last. But they came along at a time when communication technology, transportation technology, and weapons technology allowed them to be more harmful than they would have been at other points in history.

As a result of the widespread coverage of these and other incidents of mass bloodshed in the last century, our species entered the twenty-first century with some serious mass trepidation on our collective conscience. Ours has been dubbed an era of suspicion, an age of cynicism, and rightly so. The oft-quoted Lyotardian maxim that postmodernity is an incredulity toward metanarratives means that we tilt our heads skeptically when someone (especially a religious leader) pronounces, "There are two ways!" In response, we ask, "What's she selling? Who's he been duped by? And who are you to tell me that there are only two ways?!?"

To our current way of being, "There are two ways, one of life and one of death!" comes as a cold cup of water in the face. It smacks of religious intolerance. And yet, it must be dealt with. We must face it head-on and with all seriousness.

An Ancient Dichotomy

The ancient world was notoriously dualistic. Plato, the preeminent philosopher of all time, lived at the turn of the fourth century BC. In his writings, he often quoted his teacher, Socrates, who denied the reality of the material world and suggested that what human beings experience as physical reality is really just a shadow of the spiritual world; spirit, for Socrates, is good and noble and virtuous, while physicality and materiality betray evil and ignorance. The influence of Plato and Socrates on all philosophy and theology since cannot be overstated, nor can their metaphysical dualism. It has led to entire religions based on the ideas that a human being's goal should be to shed all materiality and enter the realm of pure spirit—like Manichaeism, the religion of St. Augustine prior to his conversion, which taught that all things red (like meat) are evil and things green (like vegetables) are good.

Gnosticism has always been the main challenge to Christianity from within, since most forms of Christianity are rife with Platonic influence, and dualism is Gnosticism's stock in trade. Plato introduced the term *Demiurge* in the Timeus to describe a divine Creator energy, the author of the material world. This idea was taken and expanded in later centuries and, though condemned by Neoplatonists like Plotinus, it gained traction as Gnosticism expanded. At its core, Gnosticism teaches that the material world is bad and the spiritual world is good, and there are just enough statements from Paul like, "And so, brothers and sisters, I could not speak to you as spiritual people, but rather as people of the flesh, as infants in Christ," for Gnostics to find a foothold in the New Testament.

Early in the development of Christianity, the legacy
of Gnosticism challenged the young faith. Marcion (AD
85–160) was a prominent theologian in the years just
after the writing of the Didache. As he read the stories
of Yahweh in the Hebrew Scriptures and the stories of
Jesus from the nascent Gospel accounts, they didn't
jibe. By the middle of the second century AD, he was
teaching that the God of the Hebrew Scriptures was, in
fact, the Demiurge, an evil, legalistic deity who hated
humankind and thus saddled humans with an inordinate
amount of laws. Jesus, however, was descended from
a loving, graceful Father God who loved humanity
and exuded compassion. As a result of his theological
beliefs, Marcion established a Bible that excluded the
entire Old Testament and some of the New and included
his own Gospel and some of Paul's letters. Although
he was the first famous heretic to be excommunicated
from the church in 144, he returned to his homeland in
Asia Minor and established a network of churches that
would rival the proto-Catholic church headquartered
in Rome for at least a century. And Marcion's influence
was seen in the church long after that.

But the early church's rejection of Marcion did not mean
a rejection of dualisms. You've probably already noticed
echoes between the Didache:

> There are two ways, one of life and one of death!
> and there is a great difference between the two ways.

and these words from Jeremiah:

> Thus says the Lord: See, I am setting before you the way
> of life and the way of death.

and then this from Jesus:

> Enter through the narrow gate; for the gate is wide and
> the road is easy that leads to destruction, and there are
> many who take it. For the gate is narrow and the road is
> hard that leads to life, and there are few who find it.

In fact, we see a lot of parallels between the first section of
the Didache and the Sermon on Mount, from which Jesus'
quote about the narrow gate is taken. But before we look
forward to Jesus and the Didache, let's look back at Israel.

Judaism between the Testaments

One is hard-pressed to find in the Hebrew Scriptures many
passages that presage, "There are two ways," and, "Enter
through the narrow gate." Indeed, we can find sayings like
this in the book of Proverbs,

> Do not enter the path of the wicked,
>   and do not walk in the way of evildoers.

Avoid it; do not go on it;
> turn away from it and pass on.
For they cannot sleep unless they have done wrong;
> they are robbed of sleep unless they have made
> someone stumble.
For they eat the bread of wickedness
> and drink the wine of violence.
But the path of the righteous is like the light of dawn,
> which shines brighter and brighter until full day.
The way of the wicked is like deep darkness;
> they do not know what they stumble over.

But Ecclesiastes, also attributed to King Solomon, is a book famous for its ambivalence about walking the righteous path. While the Old Testament is rife with exhortations to upright moral behavior and the laws that enforce said behavior, it does not generally speak of the human condition as one of dualisms, in the metaphors of two paths or two ways. Much of this is rooted in the fact that the Hebrew Scriptures were written for a discrete people group—the nation of Israel—and the choice as to whether one was or was not a follower of Yahweh was rather irrelevant. Instead, the Old Testament writers were more concerned about the Hebrews being *better* followers of Yahweh.

But much had changed in what Christians call the intertestamental era—the time between the end of the

Old Testament and the beginning of the New. In the approximately four hundred years between the lives of Malachi and Jesus, the conquests of Alexander the Great led to the primacy of the Greek language across the empire, resulting in, among other things, the translation of the Hebrew Scriptures into that language (the Septuagint), and the spread of Hellenistic philosophy. The Jews then enjoyed a century of self-rule before once again being overtaken by an empire—this time, the Romans.

Also in those four centuries, synagogue worship—which would foreshadow house church worship—began, and Jews began using Aramaic as their primary spoken language. The politico-religious factions of Pharisees, Saducees, Essenes, and Herodians, with whom Jesus often dealt, developed during the intertestamental period as well.

In general, it was an epoch in which some of the most Hebraic elements of Judaism were diluted, and Judaism itself shifted to a more diverse and, one might even say, globalized religion. Non-Hebrews were converting to Judaism, and the religion itself was moving outside of Israel and into more Hellenized territories, like the Syrian border town in which the Didache was composed and lived.

"There are two ways" had become a common thread by the time of Jesus and the Didache; it is a phrase used in several other early Christian documents, and it seems to originate with an older Jewish document. In fact, the Didache and the Sermon on the Mount seem to rely on a font of wisdom highly valued in first-century Judaism.

That's not to say that Judaism was diluted beyond recognition by the time of the Didache—just that it had changed—or that elements of Judaism aren't prominent therein. In fact, the very first component of the "way of life" is supremely Jewish.

A Long History of God Loving

Shema Yisrael Adonai Eloheinu Adonai Echad.

So begins the Shema, the most important prayer in Judaism: "Hear, O Israel. The Lord is our God. The Lord is one." It's importance cannot be overstated—the Shema is to Jews what John 3:16 is to many Christians.

The prayer, taken from the books of Deuteronomy and Numbers, professes God's unity and kingship, commands love for God, and exhorts love for others as well. This is it in its entirety:

Hear, O Israel: The Lord is our God, the Lord alone. [Blessed be the Name of His glorious kingdom for ever and ever.] You shall love the Lord your God with all your heart, and with all your soul, and with all your might. Keep these words that I am commanding you today in your heart. Recite them to your children and talk about them when you are at home and when you are away, when you lie down and when you rise. Bind them as a sign on your hand, fix them as an emblem on your forehead, and write them on the doorposts of your house and on your gates.

If you will only heed his every commandment that I am commanding you today—loving the Lord your God, and serving him with all your heart and with all your soul—then he will give the rain for your land in its season, the early rain and the later rain, and you will gather in your grain, your wine, and your oil; and he will give grass in your fields for your livestock, and you will eat your fill. Take care, or you will be seduced into turning away, serving other gods and worshiping them, for then the anger of the Lord will be kindled against you and he will shut up the heavens, so that there will be no rain and the land will yield no fruit; then you will perish quickly from the good land that the Lord is giving you.

You shall put these words of mine in your heart and soul, and you shall bind them as a sign on your hand, and fix them as an emblem on your forehead. Teach them to your children, talking about them when you are at home and when you are away, when you lie down and when you rise. Write them on the doorposts of your house and on your gates, so that your days and the days of your children may be multiplied in the land that the Lord swore to your ancestors to give them, as long as the heavens are above the earth.

The Lord said to Moses: Speak to the Israelites, and tell them to make fringes on the corners of their garments throughout their generations and to put a blue cord on the fringe at each corner. You have the fringe so that, when you see it, you will remember all the commandments of the Lord and do them, and not follow the lust of your own heart and your own eyes. So you shall remember and do all my commandments, and you shall be holy to your God. I am the Lord your God, who brought you out of the land of Egypt, to be your God: I am the Lord your God.

It can be said that these verses, this prayer, compose the very heart of Judaism, and what became Christianity. While the orders to add fringes to clothing as a reminder seem odd to those of us who aren't Jewish, we surely recognize the statements about God's oneness, about the love and honor that is due to God, and about God's steadfast love to Israel in bringing them out of bondage.

These sentiments are echoed throughout the New Testament:

> Jesus: "The first [commandment] is, 'Hear, O Israel: the Lord our God, the Lord is one; you shall love the Lord your God with all your heart, and with all your soul, and with all your mind, and with all your strength.' The second is this, 'You shall love your neighbor as yourself.' There is no other commandment greater than these."
> Jesus: "The father and I are one."
> Paul: "Yet for us there is one God, the Father, from whom are all things and for whom we exist, and one Lord, Jesus Christ, through whom are all things and through whom we exist."

In another spot, in fact, Paul uses the Shema as the basis for a theological argument about the acceptance of Jesus and the gospel among the Gentiles. He writes, "For we hold that a person is justified by faith apart from works prescribed by the law. Or is God the God of Jews only? Is he not the God of Gentiles also? Yes, of Gentiles also, since God is one; and he will justify the circumcised on the ground of faith and the uncircumcised through that same faith." In other words, the oneness of God, as proclaimed in the Shema, means that non-Jews don't have to convert to Judaism in order to become Christian, for that would mean that God is only God for the Jews.

Now, with the importance of the Shema in mind, consider again the first line of the way of life in the Didache: "First, you shall love the God who made you." It's no exaggeration to say that everything else in the Didache flows from this headwater.

A Rule of Gold

When Jesus restated the Shema, as recorded in the Gospel of Matthew, he was responding to a query from a pharisaical lawyer. "What," his inquisitor asked, "is the greatest commandment?" Jesus responded with the Shema, but he didn't stop there. He went on to say that the second command is, "Love your neighbor as yourself." The two—love of God and love of others—have been inextricably joined ever since.

We call it the "Golden Rule." Moral philosophers call it the "ethics of reciprocity." And it's found in virtually every religious system in history. The Didache community, by placing the Golden Rule at the top of their discipleship manual, stands in a rich tradition of faithful and religious communities who consider benevolent reciprocity to be the hallmark of ethics. As with the command to love God, the exhortation to love one's neighbor as oneself can really be seen as the font from which the rest of the Didache's teachings flow.

This stood in contrast to the ethics of the Roman Empire which was, depending on one's social standing, either "kill or be killed" or "live and let live." Acting with benevolence toward other human beings in an imperial system only makes sense if it benefits the benevolent party. Self-sacrifice is not rewarded.

One might easily say the same about our world today—in fact, the Cymbrogi do. They see much of the consumerism in our world standing at odds with the Didache's call for reciprocal benevolence. And their community, though small, has been shaped mightily by this standard. One member of the community, for example, had held a secret for many years—one that he wanted to share, but was afraid that it would reflect poorly on him in the group. When he did talk about it, he was amazed at the openness and acceptance among the Cymbrogi. As you might guess, he has been much more comfortable and open in the group ever since.

Interestingly, however, the Didache's version of the ethic of reciprocity is stated in the negative—do not do to another what you would not want done to you—whereas Jesus states it in the positive, both in Matthew's Sermon on the Mount ("In everything do to others as you would have them do to you; for this is the law and the prophets") and in Luke's Sermon on the Plain ("Do to others as you would have them do to you"), as well as in the dialogue with the pharisee quoted above. And this brings us to an interesting question about the sources that the Didache community used when they stitched this manual together, for both this verse and many others sound a lot like Jesus' words, but not quite exactly the same.

The scholarly consensus is that a mysterious document, which they call "Q," was a compilation of many of Jesus' sayings. New Testament scholars believe that Matthew and Luke used Q when they composed their Gospels, because about one quarter of the material in their Gospels is shared but is not found in Mark, the other synoptic Gospel. Scholars have hypothesized that the shared content comes from a document that they named after the German word *quelle* ("source"). Since the wording in the shared passages is often identical, Q was likely a document written in Greek, and scholars can roughly recreate the long-lost Q document by listing the material common to Luke and Matthew but not found in Mark. And what they get is many of Jesus' sayings, but no mention of miracles, the disciples, crucifixion, or resurrection.

It seems very likely that this opening portion of the Didache is also reliant upon Q. While other early Christian documents (1 and 2 Clement, the Shepherd of Hermas, the Martyrdom of Polycarp, and the Gospel of Thomas) also have material that seems to come from Q, none has an extended section like Didache 1:3–2:1, which presumably comes directly from Q. The question remains whether the compiler(s) of the Didache used Matthew and Luke in a harmonized form, or used Q in a way similar to the authors of those Gospels. The latter seems more likely, which, in turn, indicates that we should posit an earlier date for the Didache.

So why am I going on about these details of textual criticism? I have a good reason; namely, if the opening of the Didache does indeed come from Q, then these are the words of Jesus:

> Bless those who curse you, and pray for your enemies, and fast for those who persecute you. For what reward is there for loving those who love you? Do not the heathens do the same? But you should love those who hate you, and then you shall have no enemies.
> Abstain from fleshly and bodily lusts:
> If someone strikes your right cheek, turn the other also, and be perfect. If someone forces you to go one mile, go two. If someone takes your cloak, give also your coat. If someone takes from you what is yours, don't ask for it back. You really cannot.
> Give to every one who asks you, and don't ask for it back. The Father wants his blessings shared.

Happy is the giver who lives according to this rule, for that one is guiltless. But the receiver must beware; for if one receives who has need, he is guiltless, but if one receives not having need, he shall stand trial, answering why he received and for what use. If he is found guilty he shall not escape until he pays back the last penny. However, concerning this, there is a saying: "Let your alms sweat in your hands until you know to whom to give them."

The Didache doesn't format these passages as quotes, as Matthew and Luke do. Instead, they are referred to simply as the "teachings" or "sayings" (*didache*). And yet, while they are not directly attributed to Jesus, it seems clear from the context and from the parallels to Matthew and Luke (and, most probably, to Q) that we should read them as the catechumens of the Didache community read them: teachings directly from Jesus.

The Way of Life

The first time I talked about the Didache to Trucker Frank of the Cymbrogi, he made an interesting comment to me. "By the time of the church councils, even by Ignatius, all of the concentration was on ortho*doxy*—right belief," he said, "But in the Didache, the focus is ortho*praxy*—how you live." He went on, "The value here is what people do with their resources, not what comes out of their mouths. There are serious consequences in the Didache around what you do with your resources, and our group has been *affected* by this."

Right off the bat, the way of life is distinguished by action: bless those who curse you; pray for your enemies; and, a command not found in the Gospels, fast for those who persecute you. Do these things, says the Didache, and you'll have no enemies.

Since we don't actually know much about the initial readers of the Didache, we have to go with some hunches and assumptions. It seems likely that this handbook on the Christian life was given to new converts to Christianity, those who were going through the ancient process of catechesis. In the first centuries of the church, a convert to Christianity was not baptized immediately after making a profession of faith. Instead, there was a yearlong process of training and teaching, during which the catechumen would have a mentor in the faith and learn the ways of Christianity. At the end of the year, on the night before Easter, the convert would stay up all night, keeping vigil. At dawn, the catechumens were baptized and then brought into the church, where with great celebration they received communion for the first time and had a drop of milk and honey placed on their tongues, representing the Promised Land of heaven. Then, and only then, did a person go from being a catechumen to being a full-fledged Christian.

This is what we know of conversion to Christianity in the third and fourth centuries. While we're less sure of the process a century earlier, at the time of the Didache, we can imagine that it contained the seeds of this later practice, though it was surely more primitive. Although life in the ancient world was quite different than life today— no public schooling, no adolescence to speak of—the late teens and early twenties were still the time that many people made their religious choices for life. Three centuries later, a young man named Augustine left his hometown of Thagaste to study rhetoric in Carthage. There, he forsook the Christianity of his mother and converted to the neo-Platonic religion, Manichaeism. In his twenties, Augustine left Manichaeism and embraced the skepticism of the "New Academy" movement; and at thirty-two he famously and dramatically converted to Christianity. While St. Augustine is surely a unique figure, he also exemplifies the fact that despite all of the differences between his world and ours, young adulthood is forever a time of spiritual searching and discovery.

So we can imagine a young adult, maybe twenty years old, who lives in a rural village on the Syrian border at the beginning of the first century AD (of course, to her the year would have been named after the Roman consuls and unnumbered). She'd visited the closest major city, Antioch, about a day's journey away, enough times to know that a new sect of Judaism that followed a Galilean messiah had gained a foothold in that city. And she also knew that one of the two synagogues in her own town had converted to following this messiah.

In fact, one of her friends belonged to the Nazarene synagogue, and he regularly invited her to join him. But our young woman is not Jewish. She and her parents worshiped the many household—or hearth—gods common to citizens in the Roman Empire. Plus, of course, there was the cult of the emperor to uphold, for which you had to at least *act* like you believed Caesar to be divine. But what the young woman's friend has told her about his faith is compelling: it's based primarily on the love of and for a singular God, rather than a fear of the gods' retribution for lack of faithfulness. And the rate with which this religion is spreading also captures her attention—several more of her friends have recently joined.

So she decides to visit his synagogue with him. Once. And then she went back. And as she attended more and more frequently, so did more and more non-Jews like her, all are rapidly converting to the Way.

And, like them, the young woman, too, decides to embrace the religion of Jesus Christ.

A Handbook for the Apprentice

Having made clear her intention to become a "Christian"—that's what they're called in Antioch—the leaders of the synagogue in her town pairs the young woman up with a mentor, an older woman who has been following Jesus for a few years. This person will shepherd the new convert through the training that ultimately leads to her baptism on Easter morning. And, in her first meeting with her mentor, she is shown a handbook, a manual, which will be her guide into her new faith. It's called "The Teaching" or "The Training"—in her language, it's called the Didache.

Imagine looking at that little document for the first time. It's likely that the Didache community had only one copy—and, remember, they had no copies of the Bible; at most, they might have had one Gospel and a letter or two from Paul or Peter, but even that is unlikely. This was it.

Maybe the young woman and her mentor, along with a few others, gathered one or two evenings a week to hear the Didache read aloud. Read straight, it takes less than twenty minutes, but one of the leaders of the synagogue would stop every few lines to add some commentary. In Judaism, this was (and is) called midrash, a homiletical method of studying and commenting on texts comparatively. Midrash was coming to the fore of synagogue life during the second half of the first century, at the very time that the Didache was compiled. For midrash, a rabbi would read a portion of scripture and then seek a deeper meaning by citing other scripture and commenting on commonsense wisdom, law, and history. In many cases, one line of scripture became the springboard for a long philosophical exhortation.

It's not unreasonable to assume that the leader of the Didache community employed this same method as he read the Didache to the gathered converts and their mentors—maybe even to the entire community. Were you a Greek-speaking Jewish convert, the allusions to the Shema would have been immediately obvious, but if you were converting from paganism, you would have needed familiarization with Jewish customs and texts to recognize the resonance between the way of Yahweh followed by Jews and the Way of Jesus followed by Christians.

Line by line, exhortation by exhortation, the Didache was read. Maybe some in the community committed it to memory. Since they didn't have a copy to take home, all they took with them at the end of the night was what they could remember.

What was expected of a new convert by the community was an apprentice-like attitude toward the Teaching. In fact, *didache* can be translated "teaching" or "training," and throughout the Didache it's clear that, whereas we think of "teaching" as the mastery of intellectual content, this teaching is concerned with learning a new way of life.

Maybe the corollary in our day is the quickly vanishing practice of apprenticeship. Back when most people lacked schooling and were involved in trade labor, apprenticeship was the primary means of learning a trade. For centuries, a young man would be trained to be a blacksmith, cobbler, or carpenter by apprenticing to a master of the trade. Young women were taught to be seamstresses or a midwives in the same learning-by-doing manner. To this day, electricians in the United States are trained in a five-year apprenticeship program that's about 10 percent classroom learning and about 90 percent on-the-job training.

Before Christianity became doctrinalized by Ignatius and his theological heirs, conversion to the new faith was much more along the lines of apprenticeship. This was especially to combat the accusation that Christianity was another Gnostic cult. Mystery cults were popular in the first-century empire. In Pompeii, an Italian town frozen in time by the AD 79 eruption of Mount Vesuvius, there are frescoes that depict initiation into the mystery cults of Isis and Dionysus, and the militant cult of Mithras was also widespread.

Nascent Christianity had mysteries of its own, including baptismal initiation and the regular eating of the Savior's "flesh" and the drinking of his "blood," which led some to portray the faith as a new mystery cult. Christians, however, fought the stigma associated with the mystery cults and attempted to bring as much as they could into the open without inviting persecution. As the Didache shows, Christianity was not about learning an elaborate secret knowledge (like Gnosticism) or enduring a horrific initiation (like the cult of Dionysus), but about a way of life that was fundamentally concerned with love of God, love of others, self-control in matters of sex and money, and orderly worship.

In other words, the new Christians had nothing to hide.

The First Commandment

So what *are* the "two ways," according to the Didache community? The Teaching begins with two commandments—the Shema-like love of God, and the Golden Rule–like love of neighbor.

> There are two ways, one of life and one of death!
> and there is a great difference between the two ways.
> The way of life is this:
> First, you shall love God who made you. And second,
> love your neighbor as yourself, and do not do to another
> what you would not want done to you.

In what follows, the second commandment is explicated clearly with the introduction, "The second commandment of the teaching is this . . . " but the first commandment has no similar foreword. Instead, we read, "The meaning (*logon*) of these sayings (*didache*) is this," followed by exhortations, many of which parallel the Sermon on the Mount directly. We are led to believe that these first admonishments are the way that one loves the God who made us.

Noticeable are the phrases, however, that are not in the Gospels' versions of Jesus' sermons. For instance, Jesus encourages us to pray for our enemies, and even to revel in persecution because it augurs a reward in heaven. But the Didache takes the love of enemy one step further than Jesus does in the gospel accounts when it bids the believer to "fast for those who persecute you."

This may be another indication that the Didache was utilizing sources different from, but available at the same time as, those used for writing the canonical gospels. The practice of fasting had deep roots in God's people, being commended as far back as Moses. About six hundred years before the Didache, the book of Isaiah made it clear that fasting was connected to justice:

> Is not this the fast that I choose:
>> to loose the bonds of injustice,
>> to undo the thongs of the yoke,
> to let the oppressed go free,
>> and to break every yoke?

Is it not to share your bread with the hungry,
    and bring the homeless poor into your house;
when you see the naked, to cover them,
    and not to hide yourself from your own kin?
Then your light shall break forth like the dawn,
    and your healing shall spring up quickly;
your vindicator shall go before you,
    the glory of the Lord shall be your rearguard.
Then you shall call, and the Lord will answer;
    you shall cry for help, and he will say, Here I am.

And yet here, in the Didache, fasting accrues not with what we would usually consider Old Testament justice (taking an eye for an eye, evening the playing ground with your persecutor, and the like) but instead forsakes meting out "justice" for pure grace. A sacrificial act on behalf of the persecutor may, in fact, fulfill the very kind of justice hoped for by Isaiah: seeing the persecutor as the one in need of grace. Seen through the Isaiahic lens, the persecutor is one with the oppressed, hungry, and naked.

This stance isn't merely ideological. It's pragmatic, for the Didache promises that if you love those who hate you, "you shall have no enemies." Surely this posture is noble, but is it also effective? History is rife with examples of those who've sacrificed on behalf of their enemies and ended up sainted. They've also often ended up martyred, a fate that was not unknown at the time of the Didache. In fact, martyrdom was a very real possibility at the end of the first century and beginning of the second, so the promise that you would have no enemies could have been either (1) a holdover from the older Jewish document on which the opening section of the Didache was based, or (2) a nod to the apocalyptic conclusion of the teaching. In either case the poignancy of the call to fast for your enemies cannot be ignored.

Money, which we'll consider more thoroughly in the next chapter, also figures prominently in the first commandment. What you do with what you have is a leading indicator of your love for the God who made us. The key to this connection is the line, "The Father wants his blessings shared," for the God *who made you* is also the author of the blessings you have received. And God expects that we will be just as generous with others as he has been with us.

The Second Commandment

"The heart of God on paper." That's what came out of Trucker Frank's mouth once when we were reading this part of the Didache together. It's taken me some time to figure out what he meant by that, since this list at first seems like little more than a list of moral prohibitions. The inventory of sins is downright distasteful, cataloguing some of the most heinous acts that humans can perpetrate upon one another. There's the usual suspects of murder, adultery, stealing, coveting, greed, and bearing false witness. But also on the list are witchcraft, magic, and double-tonguedness, and then comes the really putrid stuff: sexual corruption of boys and murder of children.

(This last sin, commonly translated as "abortion" in the Didache 2:2h, deserves a special note, especially because of the political ramifications of that word in our world today. Strictly speaking, there was no specific word for "abortion" in Greek, the language of the Didache. The word here, *phthora*, means "destruction" or "corruption"— just a few lines earlier, the same root word is used in verse 2c, "do not corrupt boys [*paido-phthoreseis*]." Thus, the literal translation of this line is, "You shall not murder a child in destruction, neither the born will you kill." That seems to leave two possibilities for translation of this phrase. On the one hand, it probably means the abortion of a not-yet-born child, which would make sense of the next clause about killing the already-born. If *born* is translated "newly born," this reading makes even more sense. And, indeed, abortion was practiced in the ancient world, dating back to at least sixteenth-century BC Egypt. Even Hippocrates, the father of medicine, specifically mentions abortion in his fourth-century BC oath—"I will not give a lethal drug to anyone if I am asked, nor will I advise such a plan; and similarly I will not give a woman a pessary to cause an abortion"— and he prescribes how to safely perform an abortion in his

Corpus. In both cases, he uses the same word, *phthora*, as the Didache. On the other hand, the phrase could also mean to prohibit the all-too-common practice of "exposure"; that is, leaving an unwanted infant to die in the elements immediately after birth. In either case, the Didache affirms the Christian moral stance against abortion and/or exposure in opposition to the common practice of the day.)

When I later asked Frank what he meant about the heart of God on paper, he pointed to the last verse of this chapter: "Hate no one; correct some, pray for others, and some you should love more than your own life." This, said Trucker Frank, is the cornerstone verse of the entire Didache.

The assumption, he continued, is that persons engaged in all of the practices mentioned in the previous litany were involved in the young church to which the Didache was written. There were adulterers and fornicators and thieves and gossips—indeed, why else would these sins have been mentioned if those people weren't a part of the community? But what's most significant, at least in the eyes of Frank and his fellow Cymbrogi, is that the Didache does not teach that these sinners should be kept out of the assembly. To the contrary, the command to "hate no one" seems clearly to be pointing at the previous list:

Don't hate the murderer,
and don't hate the adulterer;

don't hate the one who corrupts boys

or the one who has illicit sex;

don't hate the thief, magician, or witch;

don't hate the abortionist or murderer of children.

And don't hate those who swear, lie, gossip, or lack forgiveness.

Don't hate the double-tongued, covetous, greedy, hypocritical, malicious, or arrogant.

Instead, correct them, pray for them, and some, love with a love that you didn't even know you had.

What the Didache doesn't say is that the community should shun or excommunicate those who commit the forbidden sins. In fact, "correct some, pray for others, and some you should love more than your own life" makes plain that the worst sinners should be showered with the most love. The obvious parallel comes from Matthew 18, in which Jesus instructs his disciples that in their group, one who sins should first be confronted by an individual, then by the community leaders, and ultimately by the entire community. If the sinner refuses to abandon the unrighteous behavior, Jesus teaches, "let such a one be to you as a Gentile and a tax-collector." While that sentence has long been used to ostracize sinners from the church, if we take a minute to think about how Jesus treated tax-collectors and sinners, it becomes clear that Jesus was not advocating excommunication but rather hospitality toward the sinner. "Hate no one" is the guiding premise of the community; their tag line; their mission statement.

That, says Trucker Frank, is the heart of God on paper.

Thoughts from Trucker Frank

A few of the Cymbrogi are former pastors—they're versed in studying the Bible. That's what they were taught at Bible college and seminary, and that's what they did to earn their living as preachers. But one of the things that has struck them about the Didache is that the intellectual *study* of the teaching is not what's emphasized. In fact, it's not even mentioned. Instead, the focus is on *living* the teaching. "The Didache teaches a faith of love," says Frank. "Love beyond any capacity that we have as normal people."

So the Cymbrogi were attracted to the Didache, to the unadulterated love that it teaches. "We were attracted to the simplicity of it," Frank told me. "One of our group said that a lot of people in church spend a lot of time correcting each other these days, but in order to correct another person in love, you really have to know that person. Only then, she told us, can you practice the kind of community that the Didache teaches." Surely churches all over the world and throughout the ages have struggled with this very element of community life. "Tough love" can all too easily cross over into a judgmental and sinful nature. At least for the Cymbrogi, the Didache has offered an example of love that binds rather than divides their community.

They've also taken the apprenticeship model to heart. Frank leads a group on how to read the Bible in Greek, and that serves as a type of mentoring experience for those new to the community and new to the Way of Jesus. One of the emphases of the Cymbrogi, as a result of the Greek reading group, is that all followers of Christ should spend some time getting into the original languages.

Questions for Reflection, Study, and Discussion

1. Why do you suppose that the Golden Rule is taught by virtually all religions? Does it have more significance for you in the positive ("Do unto others . . . ") or the negative ("Don't do unto others . . . ")?

2. How has your reading of the Didache influenced the way you think about the words *love* and *Christian?*

3. Looking back over the two thousand years of church history, think about times when the church has succeeded at nurturing the Way of Life and love in its members, and times when it has failed. What has led to the good times and the bad times?

4. Have you had a mentor in the faith or ever apprenticed under someone? How has that experience shaped your understanding and practice of Christianity?

5

Sex, Money, and Other Means of Getting Along

Sex and money are age-old human concerns and, as such, topics of scrutiny in every religion. The early Christianity of the Didache is no exception.

It takes some work for us to put ourselves into a first-century mindset when it comes to money, so we'll get to that next. Sex, on the other hand, isn't much of a problem.

Jesus famously said that if you look at a woman with lust in your heart, you have, for all intents and purposes, committed adultery. Jimmy Carter famously told *Playboy* magazine that, by that measure, he'd committed the sin. The Didache echoes Jesus' sentiment when it says: "My child, don't be lustful, for lust leads to illicit sex. Don't be a filthy talker or allow your eyes a free reign, for these lead to adultery." And that's not the only time that the Didache mentions sex. It comes up over and over.

A Sexual Culture Clash

Sex goes way back. I guess that goes without saying.

One thing that's difficult for us in the modern, affluent West is to remember that everything in the ancient world was much more out in the open than we're used to. In our world, a person may not see a dead body until young adulthood, and then only neatly coiffed in a casket, bedecked with a spray of flowers, with gentle music playing in the background. Two millennia ago, long before funeral homes and modern embalming, even the youngest children would have been well acquainted with corpses. Just as they were with their neighbors' excrement, which flowed in the gutter outside the front door. In Pompeii, raised steppingstones allowed pedestrians to cross the street without finding themselves ankle-deep in human and animal dung.

Pompeii was also rife with erotic art, so much, in fact, that the eighteenth century archaeologists who excavated the site were shocked at the sexual libertinism of the ancient world. As they dug away 1,700-year-old ash and rock, they found what they considered to be obscene frescoes depicting fertility gods with phalluses so large that they required slings; advertisements for a brothel showing several people involved in various heterosexual and homosexual sex acts; and similar paintings from the public baths. So much did the prurience of the ancients antagonize the prudishness of the Victorians that the latter hid away many of their discoveries, some of which were made public only as recently as 2000.

Throughout the Roman Empire, however, these frescoes were commonplace. A god with an enlarged phallus was not seen as overly erotic but as a sign that the home in which it was found had prayed to that god for fertility. The painting of a penis on a wall wouldn't have been greeted with a snigger but with a smile of understanding.

Public baths, one of the great public works of the Roman Empire, were visited daily by many citizens of the empire. In the nude, a person would stay for an hour or more, bathing, wrestling, lifting weights, and socializing with friends and neighbors. And, if the frescoes in the Pompeiian baths are any indication, public sex was not uncommon.

Marriage, too, was quite different in the ancient world. Bisexuality was customary and accepted, the most common being pederasty—a sexual relationship between a man and a boy, or, less frequently, between a woman and a girl. Meanwhile, the adults in these relationships were also in heterosexual marriages. Having various sex adult partners, even while married, was not frowned upon. While this offends our sensibilities today, it was ordinary in the Greco-Roman world of the first century.

Judaism, however, preached a different sexual ethic—one more in sync with the eighteenth-century archaeologists. The Torah teaches that sex is a private act, to be practiced exclusively between a husband and wife (or wives!). While polygamy is not condemned in the Hebrew scriptures, many other sexual acts are, including adultery, male homosexuality, incest, bestiality, masturbation, and intercourse during menstruation.

And so, Christianity's Jewish roots and its Roman context led to an inevitable clash along the lines of sexual ethics. Jesus, held by tradition to be celibate, tightened the restrictions on divorce by teaching that husbands could not divorce their wives at will. But he had little more to say on the subjects of sex and marriage.

Paul, however, was outspoken on these subjects. In particular, he was explicit when writing to the church in Corinth, a port city notorious for its one thousand temple prostitutes. From the Corinthians, Paul demanded chastity; better still, he wrote, would it be if the Corinthians chose celibacy like himself. And, in a passage showing particular agitation with the sexual practices of the Corinthians, Paul wrote, "Do you not know that wrongdoers will not inherit the kingdom of God? Do not be deceived! Fornicators, idolaters, adulterers, male prostitutes, sodomites, thieves, the greedy, drunkards, revilers, robbers—none of these will inherit the kingdom of God. And this is what some of you used to be. But you were washed, you were sanctified, you were justified in the name of the Lord Jesus Christ and in the Spirit of our God."

So we can see how the Didache community might have been caught in this clash of civilizations. If the Didache was, as we have surmised, composed for and by a community of Hellenized Jews, then by their diverse backgrounds they embodied the very collision of traditional Jewish values and Greco-Roman customs. In this vortex, the Didache clearly sides with the former. While it lacks the outright calls for chastity and celibacy of Paul and does not mention homosexuality, it does condemn pederasty (*paido-phthoreseis*), fornication (*porneia*, which implied intercourse with prostitutes), and adultery (*moicheia*, for a married man to have sex with another woman). There is no talk of marriage in the Didache, and indeed, it would be another twelve centuries before the church would consider marriage a sacrament. But the Didache does teach an ethic of sexual chastity, of self-control, and of avoiding some of the sexual excesses with which the Hellenized converts to Christianity must have been familiar. Mostly, it seems, the Didache is concerned that some of the more libertine sexual practices of the day would lead the new believer into a maelstrom of many other sins, all of which were contrary to the teaching of the Lord.

Money Won't Slip from Sweaty Hands

According to the Didache, the Way of Life has implications for how you spend your money, too. "Give to everyone who asks you," it tells us, "and don't ask for it back." Yet, just a couple sentences later, it gives the seemingly contradictory advice that the money you have to give should stay in your hand long enough for it to sweat while you wait to find someone worthy of your charity. But maybe these sentiments aren't as incongruous as they seem.

The saying, "Let your alms sweat in your hands until you know to whom to give them," was a common proverb of the day. Three centuries later, Augustine linked it to a mistranslation of a verse from the book of Sirach, a book written in Hebrew in about 180 BC and included in the Apocrypha. That verse, Sirach 12:1, reads, "If you do good, know to whom you do it, and you will be thanked for your good deeds." Sirach then reinforces the point by stating that sinners have only evil intent and should not be given alms, so the almsgiver should be sure that the recipient is virtuous before giving a handout.

Most Didache scholars are dubious about Augustine's linkage to Sirach, but they have found the proverb about alms and sweaty palms in the writings of at least sixteen other early church fathers. Some scholars even think this verse was added later as a curb on excessive giving. But Augustine and other early churchmen repeatedly show that generous giving and discerning giving are not at odds with one another, but are in fact complementary aspects of virtuous charity.

Later in the Didache, hands are once again implicated in the act of giving: "Do not be one who opens his hands to receive, or closes them when it is time to give." That's straightforward enough, but it's followed by this curious sentence: "If you have anything, by your hands you should give ransom for your sins." To Jews who had embraced Christianity, this wouldn't have been such a strange idea. The ritual of Temple sacrifice in Judaism was linked to the forgiveness of sins, and it was usual to understand that which was given to the Temple to be in recompense for past misdeeds. To pagan converts to Christianity, this may have been a foreign idea. As they were matriculated into a community in which almsgiving was part of the rhythm of life, they must have struggled not only with forgiving themselves for past sins, but also with everything that was now expected of them. With this verse, the forgiveness for those past sins and the newfound habit of generosity are coupled, and presumably, the catechumens found solace thereby.

In the end, the overriding fiscal message in the Didache is summed up in 4:7, "Do not hesitate to give, and do not complain about it." Giving, in the Didache community was a way of life and, appropriately, was central to the Way of Life.

Bring Peace to One Another

For those of us steeped in the writings of the New Testament, the horizontality of the Didache is startling. By that I mean that the Gospels and Acts and the writings of

Paul and the apostles, while concerned with interpersonal relationships, also talk a lot about the vertical relationship between humankind and God. In the Gospels, Jesus talks often of his Father in heaven, of the heavenly mansion prepared for his followers, and of parables allegorically depicting God's love for humans. Paul wrote frequently about the nature of God and the role of Jesus as the intermediary between sinful humanity and righteous divinity. And the other epistles, like those of John, wax eloquent about love and light.

But the Didache is concerned exclusively with the horizontal, with relationships between human beings. It lacks any overt theologizing about the nature of God or humanity or sin or righteousness—these seem to be understood as implicit. As Trucker Frank pointed out to me, "In the Didache, there is no difference between the gospel and the social gospel. There is *not a word* about preaching the gospel. It's all about living the gospel." (In fact, the word *gospel* [*euangelion*] appears only four times in the Didache, once as introduction to the Lord's Prayer, and the others understood as the "good news" of Christ, but without any elaboration.)

In other words, although the Didache is surely a training manual for new converts to Christianity, there is nary a word about evangelizing others into the faith. There's a plethora of admonitions about how to treat others, but not one about preaching the word and growing the church. I can hardly imagine a handbook for new Christians today that would leave out a section on evangelism. For example, millions of people have gone through the Alpha Course, a ten-week introduction to Christianity produced by an evangelical Anglican church in Great Britain. The title of the talk in week 8? "How and Why We Should Tell Others." This isn't to disparage these programs, and books on evangelism, but simply to show the different priorities of the Didache community.

The Didache cares not for telling others about the gospel, but it cares much about bringing peace to one another, keeping an open hand to the one in need, keeping your hand of love and guidance upon your children, ruling those who serve you with gentleness, and obeying those whom you serve with modesty. These are the "commandments of the Lord," and, as far as the Didache is concerned. They *are* the gospel.

The Way of Death

At first blush, it might seem that the opening of the Didache, "There are two ways, one of life and one of death! and there is a great difference between the two ways," is meant to set up a choice for the reader. But, in fact, it is not, for the original readers were catechumens who had already embraced the Christian faith and submitted to the training process of which the Didache was the centerpiece. The Way of Life is then explicated at length, with both indicative descriptors and imperative commands.

The description of the Way of Death, on the other hand, is entirely indicative and takes up less than 20 percent the length of the Way of Life. Not necessarily an afterthought, the Way of Death is mainly a recapitulation of the litanies that were said not to be the Way of Life.

Boiled down, the Way of Death is filled with behaviors that portray a lack of fear of God—those who put their trust in themselves rather than the Lord. "In a word," this section of the Didache concludes, "the way of death is full of those who are steeped in sin. Be delivered, children, from all of this!"

Thoughts from Trucker Frank

"For me, the sections on sex and money are particularly interesting," Trucker Frank told me. "I, like Jimmy Carter, have committed adultery in many ways and places. Being a single person committed to celibacy and chastity—I do what I can, as the Didache says!" The firestorm issues of our day (gay marriage, for instance) have caused the Cymbrogi to grieve for hurting people on both sides of the issues.

They have tried, in their own little community, to foster an atmosphere of openness and understanding, especially about sexuality and money, two issues that aren't usually openly discussed in conventional church communities. Frank sums it up by saying, "We are all going to be united in a much deeper fashion in God's presence than purely physical, after all."

They've decided, for instance, that whatever their various opinions about whether gay and lesbian relationships are sinful, they will welcome all people, gay or straight, equally into their community.

When it comes to money, the Cymbrogi don't take an offering or have a budget. They do collect money as needs arise in the community, and they have given a significant amount to a local food pantry. When one of the group wondered how that pantry uses its funds, he was charged with paying a visit. He found that virtually all of the Cymbrogi's contributions go straight to help the needy without being diverted to administrative costs. "This was us letting our alms sweat in our hands before distributing them," Frank laughs.

Questions for Reflection, Study, and Discussion

1. How are our changing cultural mores regarding sexuality similar to the situation of the Didache community? What should be our response to these issues?

2. What is evangelism as you understand it? Would a person from the Didache community be considered "saved" by today's standards, based on what you have read of their beliefs?

3. How would a person from the Didache community react to the use of money if they were to visit an average church today? Has this chapter affected your thinking regarding your own personal use of resources?

6
Living Together in Community

As with just about everything else in the Didache, the word church didn't have nearly the same meaning in the first century as it does today. Whereas the English word *church* means "of the Lord," the word in the Didache and in the New Testament for church is *ekklesia*, which simply means "assembly" or "gathering." To a Greek-speaker, *ekklesia* was a happening, an event, and not a place or a discrete group of people. Literally the calling (*kaleo*) out (*ek-*) of the people for a democratic assembly, the secular use of the word dates back to fifth-century BC Athens, when men of all social classes were called to assemble and vote on legislation, decide military strategy, and elect magistrates.

Thus, *ekklesia*, today translated "church" in the New Testament and the Didache, had no inherently theological meaning when those documents were written. Or, at most, it was just beginning to take on a theological meaning with these writings.

In the setting of the Eucharist, to be discussed below, there are two references to "your *ekklesia*," as in, "Remember, Lord, your church." Whereas in the New Testament Paul used *church* to refer to a single, local gathering, and *churches* to signify multiple, networked groups, the Didache uses the singular "church" to refer to what we might today call the global church. It's also what theologians later called the church invisible or the church universal— all those who are *really* saved and are known to God alone. In any case, the Didache makes it clear that this gathering, both local and global, belongs to the Father alone.

It is very difficult for us to disabuse ourselves of the connotations that come with words that are so familiar to us. Today, we all know what the word *Internet* means, but just years ago we were reading magazine articles telling us about this new technological horizon. We were defining the word for ourselves. To try to understand the Didache in the context of its original readers, we must remember that a word like *ekklesia* meant only "gathering," not a gathering of Christians, in particular. The Didache's "gathering of the Father" carried none of the baggage—good or bad—that the term *church* has today.

On Avoiding Idol Food

The next concern of the Didache is the particular practices that constitute the rhythm of life for the gathered community. Instructions about eating sacrificial meat, baptism, the Eucharist, prayers, and welcoming wandering prophets and teachers ensue. At some points, the Didache is quite explicit, and at other points it's rather vague—for instance, one might wish that there was less ink spilled on the tests for the wanderers and a more detailed description about what, exactly, happens when the community gathers.

The brief chapter that we know of as chapter 6 of the Didache provides a segue, an interlude of sorts, between the "Two Ways" section and the "How to Do Church" section. In the prior section, the ways of life and death are written in the second person *singular*. In other words, all of the "you shalls" are addressed to a singular *you*. In the sections that follow, instructions like "you should baptize in this way" are written in the second person *plural*—"y'all should baptize in this way." Differences like this lead most scholars to surmise that the Didache really is a patchwork of several documents, stitched together for the edification of disciples in training.

Verse 6:3, notably, is in the second person *singular*: "Concerning food, do what you are able to do and be on guard against meat offered to idols, for that is to worship dead gods." So it seems to belong more to the section above—the Two Ways—than to the instructions below, which are written to a community.

In this interlude, we experience another clash of cultures. While Greeks were generally tolerant of various religions, even paying homage to foreign gods on occasion, Jews were not. Here again, the young Christian community sides with Judaism, discouraging the eating of meat previously offered to idols, albeit not outright forbidding it.

The entrance of Gentiles into the community was a problem that vexed the apostles, as well. Peter, for instance, only baptized Cornelius the Centurion after the "Sheet of Meat Incident," in which God told him that he was allowed to eat cloven-hoofed animals, forbidden by Mosaic law. In one of the turning points in the Apostolic Age, Peter's commitment to upholding the Law (Torah) was upended when God told him, "Don't consider unclean what I have made clean." It was only by divine fiat that Peter understood that the Old Testament prohibitions against eating meat previously offered to idols no longer held. And baptizing Cornelius, an uncircumcised Gentile, was just another 180-degree turn for the apostle.

This same issue came up in Jerusalem, in what is considered the first council of the church. After hearing the testimony of Barnabas and Paul, James issued the judgment of the council:

> Therefore I have reached the decision that we should not trouble those Gentiles who are turning to God,

but we should write to them to abstain only from things polluted by idols and from fornication and from whatever has been strangled and from blood. For in every city, for generations past, Moses has had those who proclaim him, for he has been read aloud every sabbath in the synagogues.

The apostles then composed a letter, written to all Gentile converts to Christianity, and sent it to Antioch (likely the closest major city to the Didache community!), the hub of Gentile conversion, where it was read to the gathered community:

The brothers, both the apostles and the elders, to the believers of Gentile origin in Antioch and Syria and Cilicia, greetings. Since we have heard that certain persons who have gone out from us, though with no instructions from us, have said things to disturb you and have unsettled your minds, we have decided unanimously to choose representatives and send them to you, along with our beloved Barnabas and Paul, who have risked their lives for the sake of our Lord Jesus Christ. We have therefore sent Judas and Silas, who themselves will tell you the same things by word of mouth. For it has seemed good to the Holy Spirit and to us to impose on you no further burden than these essentials: *that you abstain from what has been sacrificed to idols* and from blood and from what is strangled and from fornication. If you keep yourselves from these, you will do well. Farewell. (emphasis added)

It is reported in Acts that the Antiochian believers "rejoiced at the exhortation" when it was read to them.

So both the apostles and the Didache strike a middle ground: Christians can eat food that is forbidden by the Torah, but meat offered to idols is a bridge too far and should be avoided. In the end, the transition from the Two Ways to the instructions for church is summed up in Trucker Frank's second-favorite verse from the Didache, which serves as a nice, commonsense motto for those who find Paul's stridency offputting: "For if you are able to bear the entire yoke of the Lord, you will be perfect; but if you are not able, then at least do what you can."

The Didache is starting to set a tone, which we'll see continued below, of centrist pragmatism—a posture that might have benefited the church in various eras. In the last five centuries, Christians have split from one another innumerable times, leading to tens of thousands of denominations. These schisms, large and small, have been over issues of whom to baptize and how to serve communion, whether women should preach and what, exactly, is a sacrament. Similar issues face the church today.

Had we heeded the Didache's advice to "do your best" in these issues, we might not have had the ideological battles that have so hurt the proclamation of the gospel.

Of Running Water

Baptism was not unique to Christians. The practice of ritual ablution was common in Judaism as a way to cleanse yourself prior to worship. For instance, baptismal cleansing was undertaken by a woman upon completion of her menses or by a man who had been made ritually unclean by touching a corpse. The Essenes, an eschatological, ascetic Jewish sect of which some scholars think Jesus was a member, washed themselves as many as six times a day in an attempt to live in continual purity.

Uniquely Christian baptism originated with Jesus' baptism by his cousin, John. Paul went on to write that baptism represents dying and rising with Christ and the new circumcision and,

I therefore, the prisoner in the Lord, beg you to lead a life worthy of the calling to which you have been called, with all humility and gentleness, with patience, bearing with one another in love, making every effort to maintain the unity of the Spirit in the bond of peace. There is one body and one Spirit, just as you were called to the one hope of your calling, one Lord, one faith, *one baptism*, one God and Father of all, who is above all and through all and in all. (emphasis added)

The Didache does not mention when baptisms are to be performed, whether they be in the weekly assemblies, on the sabbath, or once a year on Easter. The centrality of the ritual to the community is clear, but the frequency of the rite is unclear.

In examining the Didache's contribution to the early church practice of baptism, four elements are noteworthy:

1. All Things: Prior to being baptized, the candidate is to have "all things" explained to her or him. Literally translated as "say before all these," this phrase is cryptic and a bit odd. Does it refer to the Two Ways document? If so, why does it not use the term *didache* used elsewhere? In any case, it seems to imply that baptism was only to be undertaken after a period of initiatory learning—the very content of which the Didache is.

2. Trinitarian: Jesus initiated the Trinitarian formula for baptism when he is recorded in the Gospel of Matthew commissioning his disciples after his resurrection, "All authority in heaven and on earth has been given to me. Go therefore and make disciples of all nations, *baptizing them in the name of the Father and of the Son and of the Holy Spirit*, and teaching them to obey everything that I have commanded you. And remember, I am with you always, to the end of the age" (emphasis added). That formula obviously stuck, so that a few decades later, it was clearly in force in the Didache community.

3. Type of Water: The Didache's teaching about the water to be used for a baptism is attention-grabbing, primarily because it's so different than the way that Paul wrote about baptism. We're familiar with Paul's highly theological, and even esoteric, comments on baptism. In contrast, the Didache's advice is purely pragmatic, even mundane: use flowing water if you've got it; if not, then cold water; lacking that, use warm water; and if water is hard to come by, pour a little on the head three times (implying that baptism is preferably by immersion). The advice basically mimics the advice just sentences earlier about eating idol meat: *do the best you can.* Again, the most arresting part of this tone in the Didache is how different it is from Paul's repeated calls for perfection from his readers. Reading Paul's letters, one gets the impression that he was an intense and hard-driving churchman with little patience for mediocrity. In the Didache, the tone is significantly more moderate, more accepting—one might even say, more graceful.

4. Fasting: Finally, both those to be baptized and those doing the baptizing are told to fast for one or two days prior to the ceremony. They're not ordered to, exactly, but told that they "should fast," as should any others in the community who are able. This is another aspect of the baptismal rite that's not mentioned in the biblical writings, so it gives us insight into how baptism was evolving in the decades following the apostolic age.

Baptism ended the official catechetical process and served as the entry point for the convert into the Eucharistic community, for we read later, "Allow no one to eat or drink of your Eucharist unless they have been baptized in the name of the Lord." Yet the instructions for baptism do not conclude the Didache, but stand in the middle, for the convert and the community still have much to say about the Christian life.

Fasting Regularly, Pray Thrice per Day

Accounts of fasting are scattered throughout the Old Testament, from Moses through the prophets. Jesus not only fasted as the prelude to his public ministry, but also taught about fasting. He told his followers that their fasting should not be with the ostentations of sackcloth and ashes like the hypocrites, but should be done secretly and modestly—it should be an act exclusively between an individual and God. When the Pharisees asked why his disciples didn't fast like the disciples of John the Baptizer and the Pharisees, Jesus answered cryptically,

> You cannot make wedding-guests fast while the bridegroom is with them, can you? The days will come when the bridegroom will be taken away from them, and then they will fast in those days. . . . No one tears a piece from a new garment and sews it on an old

garment; otherwise the new will be torn, and the piece from the new will not match the old. And no one puts new wine into old wineskins; otherwise the new wine will burst the skins and will be spilled, and the skins will be destroyed. But new wine must be put into fresh wineskins. And no one after drinking old wine desires new wine, but says, "The old is good."

Again, the Didache deals with the pragmatics in a way that the Bible does not. Going beyond Jesus' teaching not to pray like the hypocrites, the Didache suggests that Christians fast on different days in order to distinguish themselves. In the text, the days of the fast are relative to the Sabbath: the hypocrites fast on the second and fourth days after Sabbath; you should fast on the third day and on Sabbath preparation day.

Fasting and prayer were the key components of devotional piety for Jesus and the Didache, and they are linked for both. In the Sermon on the Mount, Jesus introduces the general concept of modest piety, teaches what has become known as the Lord's Prayer, and gives the aforementioned instructions for fasting. In the Didache, the Lord's Prayer comes after the instructions on fasting, and it appears virtually verbatim to the version in the Gospel of Matthew.

Today, this prayer is so familiar to many of us that it too often loses its potency, but it should be seen in connection with the apocalyptic section at the end of the Didache and the general eschatological mood of Christians at the turn of the second century. This prayer has the End (*eschaton*) and the Second Coming (*parousia*) in mind. The expectation was that Jesus will soon return, and this prayer was part and parcel of that expectation.

Finally, the Didache community continued the long-standing tradition of prayers at specific times throughout the day. This section ends with the simple line, "Pray this three times each day," which hearkens back to the psalmist who exulted, "Seven times a day I praise you for your righteous ordinances"; to Jesus who regularly went off to pray; and to the disciples—in the first episode after Pentecost in the book of Acts, Luke writes, "One day Peter and John were going up to the temple at the hour of prayer, at three o'clock in the afternoon." To this day, thrice daily prayers—called the Daily Office—are practiced by Christians of many varieties. And to this day, the Lord's Prayer is included in every setting of the Daily Office.

Eucharist

Nothing is more intriguing—and more out-of-step with our usual ecclesial conventions—in the entire Didache than the two sections that deal with the Eucharist. Of course, the Eucharist/Lord's Supper/Communion had not taken on nearly the advanced level of symbolism just decades after Jesus' Last Supper that it has today. It can be difficult to wrench ourselves free of our predispositions, positive and negative, about a ritual as potent as the Eucharist. But we must try.

In the Didache community, the Christians gathered weekly, and possibly daily, for a shared meal. The "cup" and the "loaf" that were consecrated with the Didache's prayer of blessing are referred to in the singular, but they were not alone on the table. Instead, they sat among a bevy of shared food, what the author of Jude calls a "love (*agape*) feast." This is reinforced in Didache 10:1, which implies that one would eat enough food at the meal to be "filled" before the concluding prayers were said. In other words, there was no distinction between the Lord's Supper and the regular church potluck. Instead, by consecrating a cup and a loaf, the entire meal was blessed by proxy. It was also less formal than most of us have experienced communion. The Didache lacks any mention of the office of pastor or priest, so the later development that only clergypersons could administer the Eucharist had not yet affected the administration of the act—that would come a few years later, when Ignatius ordered that only those selected by the bishop could pass out the elements.

The Didache's setting of the Eucharist is unique. Nothing quite like it exists in all of Christian literature, and you

might even say that, at points, it stands at odds with the
biblical versions of the Lord's Supper. As with baptism, in
order to compare and contrast the Didache's setting of the
Eucharist with the Bible's, it will be most helpful to number
our points and tackle them one by one.

1. Eucharist: In the Bible, the Eucharist is not actually
referred to as the Eucharist. The episode that served as the
genesis of the sacramental rite is called the Lord's Supper
by Paul, and it has no proper name in the Gospels. The
Gospels and Paul both use a form of the verb *eucharisteo* ("to
give thanks"), but it's not until years later that the event
itself is referred to as the *eucharistia* ("the Thanksgiving").

2. The Order: The Last Supper of Jesus with his disciples
is referenced six times in the New Testament, and only in
Luke 22 is the cup blessed before the bread. Most of us
are most familiar with a pastor or priest reiterating Paul's
words, "The Lord Jesus on the night when he was betrayed
took a loaf of bread, and when he had given thanks, he
broke it and said, 'This is my body that is for you. Do this
in remembrance of me.' In the same way he took the cup
also, after supper, saying, 'This cup is the new covenant in
my blood. Do this, as often as you drink it, in remembrance
of me.'" The Jewish custom of the day was that a cup was
blessed and passed at the beginning of a meal, and this

is probably what influenced the Didache community to reverse the traditional order—it's also another indication that they were unfamiliar with Paul's letters.

3. What's Not Mentioned: Most intriguing, however, is what's missing from the Didache's version of the Eucharist, at least for those of us versed in Paul's rendition. There is no mention of the Last Supper, of Jesus' betrayal, of sacrifice, of body or blood. For that matter, there's no reference to Jesus' death. What Paul—and we—consider most crucial to understanding the Lord's Supper, the Didache is completely lacking.

So let's turn to what *is* there, for the Didache includes a beautiful setting of the Eucharist, with wonderful blessings that many churches today would do well to implement in worship.

"First, concerning the cup," begins the liturgy, "we thank you, our Father, for the holy vine of David your servant, which you made known to us through Jesus your servant." The "holy vine" was a favorite image for Israel among the Old Testaments prophets. Isaiah, Jeremiah, Hosea, and Ezekial all made use of it. What Jesus did was open God's previously proprietary relationship with Israel to Gentiles. Thus the cup, being drunk, post-baptism, for the first time by Gentile converts, symbolizes their entry into Israel, at least spiritually.

In the world of the Didache, bread was the stuff of life—it was the staple food at every meal, thus the petition, "Give us enough bread day-by-day," in the Lord's Prayer. Baked in round, relatively flat loaves, bread was passed at a meal with each diner tearing off a piece. In the Didache's Eucharist, the broken loaf represents "the life and knowledge which you made known to us through Jesus your servant." For a Gentile convert to Christianity, Jesus proffered the knowledge of Yahweh that had been long known by Israel. For the newly baptized believer, eating a share of the Eucharistic loaf for the first time completed the months of training undertaken in the Way of Life.

The loaf also serves as an eschatological symbol: "Even as this broken bread was scattered over the hills, and was gathered together and became one, so let your church be gathered together from the ends of the earth into your kingdom." Thus, the broken bread serves a twofold purpose: both to represent the sustenance that comes with learning the Way of Life, and also to remind the eater that he or she is just one broken piece of a much bigger whole that will, someday, be put all together in God's Kingdom.

Chapter 10 of the Didache contains a truly remarkable and beautiful prayer, to be recited after the Eucharistic meal was complete. Effluent praise and thanksgiving are showered upon the holy Father, for knowledge, faith, and immortality; for food and drink—both physical and spiritual. And echoing the prayer for the church, like bread scattered across a field, to be ultimately gathered up into one, the post-Eucharist prayer asks that God gather the church from the four winds. Then, with a flourish, this section ends with a nearly breathless doxology, capping off a most profound setting of the Lord's Supper:

> Let grace come, and let this world pass away!
> Hosanna to the Son of David! If anyone is holy, let him come; if anyone is not holy, let him repent. Maranatha! Amen.

Those Pesky Visitors

The good news is that there were no television preachers in the first century. The bad news is that they seemed to have a problem with wandering prophets and teachers. So much so, in fact, that the Didache spends three times as much time on how to deal with them as it does on baptism!

The early days of Christianity were populated with itinerant charismatics who lived an ascetic and nomadic life. They depended on the Christian communities in each town to take them in and provide them with food and shelter. In return, these Spirit-filled men (and women?) would preach the gospel to those assembled.

However, this role was easily copied by charlatans and hucksters, and the fakes could be difficult to sniff out, especially for a new convert who might be especially susceptible to the wiles of a con man. So the Didache teaches discernment—generosity chastened with wisdom—when it comes to these prophets and teachers.

The overarching rule in receiving the itinerant churchmen is hospitality:

> "Let every apostle who comes to you be received as the Lord."
> "Welcome anyone coming in the name of the Lord."
> "Every genuine prophet who wants to live among you is worthy of support."

But from there the community is given many indicators by which to measure whether the wanderer is, indeed, genuine. If he overstays his welcome or asks for money or eats a "meal in the Spirit" or doesn't do what he preaches— these are sure signs that he's a false prophet.

The Didache does not abolish the role of itinerant preacher. To the contrary, the amount of space used in setting forth the guidelines for dealing with them betrays just how important these wanderers were to the early church.

Ultimately, the Didache comes down where it always does—on the side of common sense: If a prophet or teacher wanders in to your community and wants to stay, he'd better get a job. If he's unwilling to work, you should be unwilling to listen to him!

Community Leadership

In the final two sections on how to run your church, the Didache tackles reconciliation and leadership. First, in a recapitulation of Didache 4:14 ("In the gathering, confess your transgressions, and do not come for prayer with a guilty conscience"), the converts are instructed to gather on the Lord's day and confess prior to breaking bread and giving thanks. The charge is straightforward: you're really not prepared to worship unless you've cleansed your spirit of those things that you've perpetrated on your brothers and sisters in the community. The second line of chapter 14 reinforces the point, but puts the onus on every member of the community: everyone is to be on guard that reconciliation happens before worship. (And, let it be noted that the word here for "sacrifice" is *thusia*, which denotes joyous celebration, as opposed to *holókauston*, which represents a burnt sacrifice.)

And then, in the penultimate chapter, the catechumens are told how the gathering will be led and organized. The community is to appoint overseers. Although the word for "overseers," *episcopous*, is commonly translated "bishops," it's doubtful that those who held that position had yet taken on the titular authority that bishops were to be granted just a few years hence. For one thing, there's no mention of priests (*hierious*) or pastors/elders (*presbuterios*) who serve below bishops. For another, the Didache community could not have been very large, and yet they call for plural bishops. In the future, a bishop was placed over a region, and a priest or pastor led a single congregation, but in the Didache, the "bishops" led the local community, so it makes more sense for us to translate *episcopous* as "overseers" or "leaders."

And the *diakonous*, which is translated "deacons," is more appropriately translated "servant." So, what we really have is a statement that reads, "Appoint overseers for yourselves, as well as servants." Here there is no talk of one being "called" into ministry by God, but instead an appointment by a discerning community, realizing that it needs leadership in the form of overseers, and it needs people committed to doing the dirty work of the community—the organizing, clean-up, administration, and as mentioned in the book of Acts, looking after those less fortunate members of the community.

The Didache bids the community to appoint meek, honorable, truthful, and proven people to these positions, and to treat them with respect, for they, too, serve as prophets and teachers.

The ecclesial structure of the Didache community is skeletal, and it's simple:

Live reconciled lives with one another;

Confess and forgive one another;

Appoint some among you to preside over the community
and others to serve;

And treat those you've appointed with respect.

Thoughts from Trucker Frank

Frank describes the Didache as the Rosetta Stone of the New Testament, particularly helping the Cymbrogi understand the writings and teachings of Paul. "Christians have split for centuries over communion and baptism," Frank says, "and the Cymbrogi is made up of people whose denominational backgrounds reflect those splits: Baptists, Lutherans, Methodists, Catholics, and others." Frank continues, "The Didache's message that we should 'do our best' on these controversial issues have kept us from getting hung up on the things that our grandparents got hung up on."

"I am always drawn back to the miracles of the feeding of the five thousand and the four thousand when I read the Didache account of the Eucharist bread being scattered over the hills and then regathered," Frank says. "The same verbs *took, blessed, broke,* and *gave* are used by the Bible in the

Last Supper accounts and in the feeding of the multitude accounts. Interesting that when the scattered fragments were regathered in those stories, they numbered more than what was originally distributed."

Questions for Reflection, Study, and Discussion

1. How does your church practice baptism and communion? Discuss these practices compared to the Didache.

2. Why has the practice of fasting been abandoned by so many in the modern church when it was a cornerstone of the ancient church? What has been your experience with fasting?

3. Most churches today hire pastors from outside of their community of faith. Discuss the Didache's concept of leadership from within the local community and outside teachers passing through. How would the principles outlined in the Didache change the way that your church functions?

7
The End Is Nigh

I may have misled you earlier. I suggested that whether two thousand years ago or today, two topics are always popular: sex and money. I should have added a third: speculation about when and how the world will end.

Apocalypse is derived from a Greek word that means "unveiling," and apocalyptic literature was as popular in the first and second centuries as science fiction is today. It all began hundreds of years earlier, as seen in the Old Testament book of Daniel and similar visions in Ezekiel and Isaiah. Daniel is less like the other prophetic books in the Hebrew scriptures and more like a new form of literature. Whereas the previous prophetic books featured a singular prophet calling Israelites back to righteousness and holiness in God's voice, Daniel uses vivid language and imagery to portray the end of the world. In a series of four visions, Daniel writes of beasts, kingdoms, rams' horns, and a seventy-year desolation of Jerusalem.

Apocalyptic literature grew more popular during the intertestamental times, and we have dozens of examples of noncanonical literature from the period with names such as

The Testaments of the XII Patriarchs, *The Assumption of Moses*, and *The Syriac Apocalypse of Baruch*.

The mid-twentieth-century discovery of the Dead Sea Scrolls of the Qumran community has only reinforced this. A collection of about nine hundred documents placed in caves between 150 BC and AD 70, the scrolls seem to be the library of an Essene community. Along with the remnants of Old Testament books are many previously unknown apocalyptic works. In fact, the prominence of eschatological literature in the cave scrolls has led to the scholarly consensus that they belonged to the Essene sect.

So when John received a revelation while exiled on the Island of Patmos, it was not an unfamiliar way of talking about God's plans for the end of the world. The result, the book of Revelation, is surely the most widely known apocalyptic book in the world. But the Didache and many other early Christian documents were written in the same apocalyptic style.

Is the End Really Nigh?

There's a common misconception that the early Christians worshiped in the catacombs outside of Rome for fear of being caught worshiping above ground. In fact, there is no evidence that they ever worshiped as such. More probably, the earliest Christians did as their neighbors and gathered over burial plots to share memorial meals on the anniversaries of their loved ones' deaths.

What did set the early Christians apart from their fellow Roman citizens is that they did not cremate their dead. Instead, like Jews, they preferred full-body burial in expectation of the resurrection of the dead. The earliest Christians strongly believed that Jesus' return was imminent, and that the resurrection of the dead that Jesus had predicted would happen upon his return. Their belief was based on Jesus' own sayings, like this one, which follows an extended sermon about the destruction of Jerusalem and the return of the Son of Man:

> Look at the fig tree and all the trees; as soon as they sprout leaves you can see for yourselves and know that summer is already near. So also, when you see these things taking place, you know that the kingdom of God is near. *Truly I tell you, this generation will not pass away until all things have taken place.* Heaven and earth will pass away, but my words will not pass away. (emphasis added)

As the first generation of Jesus followers began to die, the early church had something of a crisis on their hands. The generation to which Jesus said these things *was* passing away, but the events of which Jesus spoke had not yet taken place. Yes, the Temple had fallen to the Romans in AD 70, and there had been arrests, persecutions, and even deaths. But they waited and waited, and Jesus didn't come back.

Their belief in Jesus' second coming, however, was not squelched. As the sixteenth chapter of the Didache testifies, first-century Christians continued to think and write about the end of time with passionate and imaginative language.

Be On Watch

As in the New Testament, the unknown moment of Jesus' return is a reason for his followers to be prepared. The catechumens of the Didache community are told to watch over their lives, safeguard their lamps, and cover their loins in expectation of the Lord's coming. They are told to gather with the community regularly and to seek the good.

"False prophets and corrupters," the very wandering ones whom they were told to test in chapter 11, are indicators that the last days are imminent. Whereas Jesus said, "Beware of false prophets, who come to you in sheep's clothing but inwardly are ravenous wolves," the Didache says that sheep will be turned into wolves. And in a chilling phrase, they are told, "love will be turned to hate." They won't be disguised, but they will actually change.

The Didache's version of the "anti-Christ" is the "world-deceiver," who will claim to be the Son of God. In another chilling phrase, he is described as doing "iniquitous things that have not been seen since the beginning of the world."

Fire!

The Didache warns of a trial, of fire, of many people perishing, and only those whose faith endures being saved. On the one hand, language like this can be very difficult for us to reconcile as modern, enlightened believers. On the other hand, think of the number of summer blockbuster movies that use apocalyptic end-of-the-world backdrops for the hero's exploits. Whether it be a killer virus, aliens, or a third world war, something deep within us seems to think that when the world does end, it will be in dramatic fashion.

The Didache's vision of the world's end really isn't that different from so many movies. With vivid images of fire, banners unfurling in the heavens, and trumpet blasts, the end of the present age happens with a flourish. But, as a seminary professor once told me, the point of Christian apocalypses like Revelation and the Didache's final chapter is simple: *God wins*. The Son of Man will return to claim those who have remained faithful to him.

And there the Didache ends, rather abruptly, with the promise that Christ will return, which will be good news for some and cause mourning among others.

Thoughts from Trucker Frank

"Be watchful. Be ready. But don't obsess." That's how Trucker Frank characterizes the final section of the Didache. Frank and his ex-brother-in-law, John, both come from "pre-tribulation rapture, millennial" versions of the end times. "Neither of us thought that we would live to see the year 2000," Frank told me. "We were sure that we would be raptured before that." The emphasis in their youth groups growing up was that you'd better be ready at all times, because if Jesus comes back and you're not ready . . . well, it won't be good. Frank even admits to having a bumper sticker on his first car that read, "In case of rapture, this car will be unoccupied."

Meanwhile, other members of the Cymbrogi were skeptical of rapture theology because of the way that it caused the people who believed it to act. As John and Frank studied, they too began to question the theology in which they were reared. Then, when they read the Didache, the lightbulb went on: "These people weren't sitting around waiting for God to rapture them out of there," Frank says. "They were doing everything they could to live in the faith and make the world a better place. They weren't concerned about *when* Jesus would come back."

Questions for Reflection, Study, and Discussion

1. When you were young, how were you taught that the world would end? How has that belief changed over the years?

2. Do you tend to be frightened by depictions of the apocalypse in Revelation and the Didache, or do you find them comforting?

Epilogue
The "Teaching"

Having spent the last year or so reading and thinking about the Didache, I have to admit that it has significantly influenced my Christian faith. To me, it represents a lost version of Christianity, and one that many of us long to get back to.

All across the United States, and all over the world, small, organic communities of faith—like the Cymbrogi—are blossoming. They are indigenous to the areas in which they are born, but they all reflect a desire to embrace a primitive Christianity, tainted neither by Constantine nor consumerism. It's happening in urban centers and on rural organic farms.

Of course, we're not the first generation to quest after a raw, primitive version of the faith. At various stages over the past two millennia, Christians have questioned the traditions of "church" and "religion" in an effort to follow Jesus more authentically. Benedict did it. Francis and Clare did it. Julian did it. So did the Shakers and the Quakers and the Jesus People.

And all along, a manual of primitive Christianity sat hidden, right in front of us.

The Didache's secrets are not as mysterious as the Gnostic writings that land skeptical professors on the bestseller lists these days. This is not a record of Jesus' exploits as a divine boy, turning clay pigeons into real ones to impress his peers at recess. No, the Didache's testimony from the first century is much simpler, and much less headline worthy. Herein lies nothing particularly controversial.

As opposed to being challenging to scholars and historians, the Didache presents a challenge to every one of us who endeavors to follow Jesus. In plain and unadorned language, it calls us to self-sacrifice, altruism, and faithfulness. We're called to love God and to love one another; to pray and fast for those who stand against us; and to give away everything we can.

Honestly, I think that for the one who has already been trying to follow Christ, the first reaction upon reading the Didache will be, "I know, I know!" For it reinforces, in clear and straightforward ways, what we already know—we should treat one another well and give ourselves over to the way of God.

How we live together, too, is implicated by the Didache. As Trucker Frank has told me, the word *church* has undergone a complete transformation in his thinking. Many things he equated with church have been washed away by the Didache. Instead, he now sees church as no more (and no less!) than a gathering of God's people, sharing wine and bread, baptizing those new in the faith, and supporting one another as they try to live by the teaching of the Lord.

Frank used to despair when he read Paul's letter to the church in Ephesus, for it commends the Ephesians to "maintain the unity of the Spirit in the bond of peace." Unity in the church seemed to Frank like some unattainable dream. But the very items of the faith that used to separate the Cymbrogi—such as whether to baptize by immersion or sprinkling—were overcome when they read the Didache as a community. There they saw one of the very earliest Christian communities saying, in effect, *do the best you can.* If you've got running water, great. If not, make do with what you have.

This is, indeed, so far removed from what we see across much of the landscape of Christianity today. Denominations are facing schism over issues of sexuality as they once did over slavery; local churches are in court with their denominations over who owns the land and who owns the building. And there is the never-ending human proclivity to sin, which results in church leaders perpetrating the worst atrocities imaginable on their congregants.

And yet there is, as I wrote above, a movement among God's people—indeed, a movement authored by God's

Spirit—to sacrificially and wholeheartedly serve Christ and one another. The Didache, I think, holds an important key to this work. By looking back to this beautiful, simple, ancient handbook, we can look forward to living Christianly in a world not so different from theirs.

The challenge to each one of us—and to each of the Christian communities in which we have placed ourselves—is whether or not to do anything about it. Our brothers and sisters in the faith who lived in the Didache community call us away from the marginalia that consumes us today. They call us to simple community in which righteous living is taught and expected, sharing life is a way of life, visiting preachers are welcomed but not given any power in the community, baptism and Eucharist are practiced regularly, and Jesus' return is expected and hoped for. Just a few activities, done well, shaped the Didache community. How can we simplify our church settings, our church language, so that our gatherings can be understood by all? How can we develop church structures that are not intimidating but welcoming, even to those who are wondering about the reality of God? The Didache is our ancient church diet manual. It reminds us that a simple diet of holiness, Eucharist, and love are the key ingredients for Christian community, and a focus on those will bring the community together in the way that Jesus prayed in John's Gospel.

There are more and more people these days who are questing after a simpler Christianity. And there may be no better way to move in that direction than using the Didache in the same way that it was originally used: as a handbook for those new to Christianity, and for those newly rediscovering it.

I will conclude by once again quoting my friend Trucker Frank, who more than anyone has helped me understand the Didache. "There are two ways," he told me, "and they are *love* and *not love*. I choose love."

About Paraclete Press

Who We Are

Paraclete Press is a publisher of books, recordings, and DVDs on Christian spirituality. Our publishing represents a full expression of Christian belief and practice—from Catholic to Evangelical, from Protestant to Orthodox.

We are the publishing arm of the Community of Jesus, an ecumenical monastic community in the Benedictine tradition. As such, we are uniquely positioned in the marketplace without connection to a large corporation and with informal relationships to many branches and denominations of faith.

What We Are Doing

Books

Paraclete publishes books that show the richness and depth of what it means to be Christian. Although Benedictine spirituality is at the heart of all that we do, we publish books that reflect the Christian experience across many cultures, time periods, and houses of worship. We publish books that nourish the vibrant life of the church and its people—books about spiritual practice, formation, history, ideas, and customs.

We have several different series, including the best-selling Living Library, Paraclete Essentials, and Paraclete Giants series of classic texts in contemporary English; A Voice from the Monastery—men and women monastics writing about living a spiritual life today; award-winning literary faith fiction and poetry; and the Active Prayer Series that brings creativity and liveliness to any life of prayer.

Recordings

From Gregorian chant to contemporary American choral works, our music recordings celebrate sacred choral music through the centuries. Paraclete distributes the recordings of the internationally acclaimed choir Gloriæ Dei Cantores, praised for their "rapt and fathomless spiritual intensity" by *American Record Guide*, and the Gloriæ Dei Cantores Schola, which specializes in the study and performance of Gregorian chant. Paraclete is also the exclusive North American distributor of the recordings of the Monastic Choir of St. Peter's Abbey in Solesmes, France, long considered to be a leading authority on Gregorian chant.

DVDs

Our DVDs offer spiritual help, healing and biblical guidance for life issues: grief and loss, marriage, forgiveness, anger management, facing death, and spiritual formation.

Learn more about us at our Web site:
www.paracletepress.com, or call us toll-free at 1-800-451-5006.

Also by Tony Jones . . .

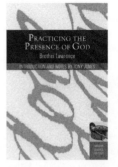

Practicing the Presence of God

ISBN: 978-1-55725-465-8
Paperback, $15.99

Brother Lawrence's *Practice of the Presence God* has stood the test of time because it chronicles the life of a very ordinary per- who became an extraordinary Christian. Through a life of humility and service, Brother Lawrence became so concentrated on God that in every moment, whether deep in prayer or peeling potatoes in the kitchen, he knew God's presence. This accessible translation is replete with enlightening background notes by Tony Jones.

You Converted Me: The Confessions of St. Augustine

ISBN: 978-1-55725-463-4 • Paperback, $16.95

Born in 354, Aurelius Augustinus became one of Christianity's greatest heroes. In these pages, Augustine lets it all spill out—from the deep trust he had in his mother, to his feelings of guilt, to his ultimate and dramatic conversion at age thirty-three. Whether you are fifteen or fifty, this edition of Augustine's *Confessions* will open up the life and wisdom of the first, famous, Christian rebel—a man whose heart was set on fire for God.

Available from most booksellers or through Paraclete Press:
www.paracletepress.com; 1-800-451-5006.
Try your local bookstore first.